1 All-Star
Student Workbook

Linda Lee

Kristin Sherman ★ Grace Tanaka ★ Shirley Velasco

Second Edition

Mc Graw Hill

Connect
Learn
Succeed™

Connect
Learn
Succeed™

ALL-STAR 1: WORKBOOK

Published by McGraw-Hill, a business unit of The McGraw-Hill Companies, Inc., 1221 Avenue of the Americas, New York, NY, 10020. Copyright © 2011 by The McGraw-Hill Companies, Inc. All rights reserved. Previous edition © 2005. No part of this publication may be reproduced or distributed in any form or by any means, or stored in a database or retrieval system, without the prior written consent of The McGraw-Hill Companies, Inc., including, but not limited to, in any network or other electronic storage or transmission, or broadcast for distance learning.

Some ancillaries, including electronic and print components, may not be available to customers outside the United States.

This book is printed on acid-free paper.

Printed in the United States of America.

5 6 7 8 9 0 QTN/QTN 1 0 9 8 7 6

Workbook

ISBN 978-0-07-719716-2
MHID 0-07-719716-X

ISE

ISBN 978-0-07-131386-5
MHID 0-07-131386-9

Vice president/Editor in chief: *Elizabeth Haefele*
Vice president/Director of marketing: *John E. Biernat*
Director of development, ESL Domestic: *Valerie E. Kelemen*
Developmental editor: *Valerie Kelemen, Laura LeDrean*
Director of sales and marketing, ESL Domestic: *Pierre Montagano*
Lead digital product manager: *Damian Moshak*
Digital developmental editor: *Kevin White*
Director, Editing/Design/Production: *Jess Ann Kosic*
Project manager: *Jean R. Starr*
Senior production supervisor: *Debra R. Sylvester*
Senior designer: *Srdjan Savanovic*
Senior photo research coordinator: *Lori Kramer*
Photo researcher: *Allison Grimes*
Digital production coordinator: *Brent dela Cruz*
Typeface: *11/13 Frutiger Roman*
Compositor: *Laserwords Private Limited*
Printer: *Quad Graphics*
Cover credit: *Andrew Lange*
Credits: The credits section for this book begins on page 154 and is considered an extension of the copyright page.

The Internet addresses listed in the text were accurate at the time of publication. The inclusion of a Web site does not indicate an endorsement by the authors or McGraw-Hill, and McGraw-Hill does not guarantee the accuracy of the information presented at these sites.

www.mhhe.com

All-Star is a four-level, standards-based series for English learners featuring a picture-dictionary approach to vocabulary building. "Big picture" scenes in each unit provide springboards to a wealth of activities developing all of the language skills. Each *All-Star* Workbook unit provides 14 pages of supplementary activities for its corresponding Student Book unit. The workbook activities offer students further practice in developing the language, vocabulary, and life-skill competencies taught in the Student Book. Answers to the Workbook activities are available in the Teacher's Edition.

Workbook Features

★ **Standards coverage complements the Student Book** for a comprehensive program covering all revised national standards: CASAS, SCANS, EFF, Florida, LAUSD, Texas, and others.

★ **Wide range of exercises** can be used by students working independently or in groups, in the classroom, with a tutor, or at home. Each unit includes several activities that allow students to interact, usually by asking and answering questions.

★ **Alternate application lessons** complement the Student Book application lesson, inviting students to tackle work, family, and/or community extension activities in each unit.

★ **Student Book page references** at the top of each Workbook page show how the two components support one another.

★ **Practice tests** at the end of each unit provide practice answering multiple-choice questions such as those found on the CASAS tests. Students are invited to chart their progress on these tests on a bar graph on the inside back cover.

★ **Crossword puzzles and word searches** reinforce unit vocabulary.

Alternate Application Lessons (Work, Family, Community)

Equipped for the Future (EFF) is a set of standards for adult literacy and lifelong learning developed by The National Institute for Literacy (www.nifl.gov). The organizing principle of EFF is that adults assume responsibilities in three major areas of life—as workers, as parents, and as citizens. These three areas of focus are called "role maps" in the EFF documentation.

Lesson 6 in each unit of the Student Book provides a real-life application relating to one of the learners' roles. The Workbook includes two alternate application lessons that expand on two of the three roles. This allows you, as the teacher, to customize the unit to meet the needs of your students. You can teach any or all of the application lessons in class. For example, if all your students work, you may choose to focus on the work applications. If your students have diverse interests and needs, you may have them work in small groups on different applications. If your program provides many hours of classroom time each week, you have the material to cover all three roles.

Contents

Identifying Countries

A Write the missing letters of the countries.

China	Vietnam	Somalia	France	Morocco
Haiti	Brazil	Colombia	Canada	Mexico

1. Col o m b i a
2. So m al i a (só' ma' li à)
3. H ai ti (hi' lià)
4. C an a d a
5. Ch i n a

6. Bra z i l
7. F r ance
8. M e x i c o
9. V i e tn a m
10. Mo r o c c o

Write the name of one more country. _____

B Complete the sentences. Write *am*, *are*, or *is*.

1. Nicoletta __is__ from Italy.
2. They __are__ from China.
3. He __is__ from Russia.
4. I __am__ from England.
5. We __are__ from Japan.
6. She __is__ from India.
7. You __are__ from Kenya.
8. Ken and I __are__ from Korea.
9. Paul and Henry __are__ from Haiti.
10. You and Ali __are__ from Morocco.
11. Eva __is__ from Mexico.

am	are	is

C Write the sentences with *you, we, they, he, she,* or *it.*

1. Victor and Carlos are from Mexico.
   They are from Mexico.

you	we	they
he	she	it

2. You and Sonia are from Brazil.
   you are from Brazil

3. Tanya is from Haiti.
   She is from Haiti

4. Laura and I are from Colombia.
   we are from Colombia

5. George is from China.
   he is from China

6. Martha and Elizabeth are from Canada.
   They are from Canada

7. Brazil is in South America.
   It is in south America

D Match the questions and answers.

Questions

1. _b_ Where are Sandra and Juan from?
2. _f_ Where are you from?
3. _e_ Where is Ed from?
4. _c_ Where are you and Tien from?
5. _a_ Where is Marie Claire from?
6. _d_ Where is your teacher from?

Answers

a. She's from France.
b. They're from Mexico.
c. We're from Vietnam.
d. She's from the United States.
e. He's from Colombia.
f. I'm from Somalia.

E Write the contractions.

1. he is   he's
2. I am   I'm
3. they are   They're
4. she is   She's
5. we are   we're
6. you are   you're

3

Unit 1: Getting Started

In the Classroom

A Write the words under the pictures.

book	chair	clock	computer	map	table

chair

table

book

clock

map

computer

B Circle the correct answers.

EXAMPLE: Where's the desk?

    A. It's on the floor.   B. It's on the wall.   C. It's on the table.

1. Where's the clock?

    A. It's on the floor.   B. It's on the wall.   C. It's on the table.

2. Where's the table?

    A. It's on the floor.   B. It's on the wall.   C. It's on the table.

3. Where's the computer?

    A. It's on the floor.   B. It's on the wall.   C. It's on the table.

4. Where's the map?

    A. It's on the floor.   B. It's on the wall.   C. It's on the table.

5. Where's the book?

    A. It's on the floor.   B. It's on the wall.   C. It's on the table. (thấy bỏ)

C Write 5 things you have in your house.

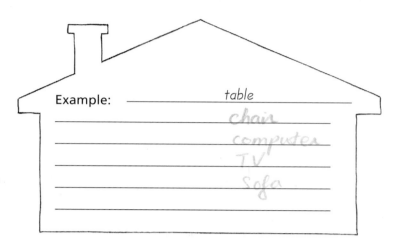

Example: _____ table _____

_____ chair _____

_____ computer _____

_____ TV _____

_____ sofa _____

_____

D Look at the picture of Rosa and Lou. Complete the sentences with *in, on, above, under,* or *beside.*

?ở trên   Lên cạnh

1. The computer is _____ on _____ the table.

2. The dog is _____ under _____ the table.

3. The table is _____ above _____ the dog. (ở bóp)

4. Rosa is _____ beside _____ Lou.

5. The pencils and pens are _____ in _____ the cup

E Answer the questions.

1. Where is your book? _____ My book is on the table _____

2. Where is your teacher? _____ My teacher is in the classroom _____

3. Where is your clock? (khót) _____ My clock is on the walls _____

4. Where is your pencil? _____ My pencil is in the bookbag _____

5

Understanding Classroom Instructions

A Match the instructions to the pictures. Write the numbers on the lines.

Students,
Sit down. _____5_____
Take out a piece of paper and a pencil. _____1_____
Open your book to page 9. _____4_____
Write your name on the piece of paper. _____2_____
Listen to the words. _____3_____
Write the words on the piece of paper. _____6_____

1.
2.
3.
4.
5.
6.

B Check the instructions the teacher writes on the board in Activity A.

EXAMPLE:

☑ Sit down.

☑ 1. Open your book to page 9.

☐ 2. Read page 10.

☐ 3. Close the window.

☑ 4. Take out a piece of paper and a pencil.

☐ 5. Repeat the words.

☑ 6. Write your name on the piece of paper.

☑ 7. Write the words on the piece of paper.

☐ 8. Ask a partner.

☐ 9. Go to the board.

☑ 10. Listen to the words.

C Write 3 instructions your teacher says in the classroom.

EXAMPLE: _____ *Take out a piece of paper.* _____

1. _____
2. _____
3. _____

D Write the numbers as words.

EXAMPLE: 10 __*ten*__

2 _____   6 _____
7 _____   4 _____
9 _____   3 _____
0 _____   1 _____
8 _____   5 _____

E Write the missing words.

EXAMPLE: six, __*seven*__, eight

1. one, two, _____
2. four, _____, six
3. nine, _____, eleven
4. seven, _____, nine
5. _____, seven, eight

F Write the plural forms of the words.

1. desk   _____
2. country   _____
3. piece of paper _____
4. word   _____
5. classroom   _____
6. page   _____
7. student   _____
8. window   _____
9. chair   _____
10. class   _____

Reporting Personal Information

A Make words from the letters.

address	~~city~~	birthplace	gender	female
male	street	state	single	married

EXAMPLE: tcyi _____ city _____

1. deerng _____ female gender. _____
2. mlefea _____ female _____
3. tteres _____ street _____
4. glensi _____ single _____
5. dsdsrae _____ address _____

B Complete the form with your information.

Application Form
(PLEASE PRINT)

_____ VAN _____   _____ LE _____   _____ TRAN _____
First Name   Middle Name   Last Name

ADDRESS: _____ 555 North Ave 4L , Fort lee, NJ 07024 _____
            Street   City   State   Zip Code

TELEPHONE NUMBER: (845) 270 - 8968 _____
                     AREA CODE

BIRTHPLACE: (li) Viet Nam _____ DATE OF BIRTH: _____ 12/07/1986 _____

GENDER: ☐ Male   ☑ Female

MARITAL STATUS: ☐ Single   ☑ Married   ☐ Divorced

OCCUPATION: _____

C Read the story. Match the information.

Her name is Cindy. Her last name is Johnson. Her address is 451 Kittridge Street, Reseda, California. Her telephone number is (818) 555-4872. She is single. Cindy is a bus driver. Her birthplace is Seattle, Washington.

Information Words	Information About Cindy
1. birthplace	a. Johnson
2. address	b. single
3. area code	c. Seattle, Washington
4. occupation	d. 818
5. marital status	e. 451 Kittridge Street, Reseda, California
6. last name	f. bus driver

D Read the story. Complete the sentences.

My teacher is from California. Her name is Rosa Lynch. She is married. Her address is 122 4th Street in Huntington Park, California. The zip code is 90255. She is a teacher at the Gardena Adult School. I am a student in her class.

1. The teacher's name is ___Rosa Lynch___.
2. Her occupation is ___teacher___.
3. Her city is ___Huntington Park___.
4. Her zip code is ___90255___.
5. Her address is ___122 4th street in Hungtington Park, CA___

E Complete the sentences with a possessive adjective or a pronoun.

1. This is my brother, Steve. ___His___ last name is Miller. ___He___ is from California. ___He___ is a student at Ridgewood.

2. My name is Edie and my husband is Ted. ___We___ are married. ___Our___ address is 9 Oak Street. ___We___ live in Florida.

3. This is Marie and Claudia. ___they___ are not married. ___they___ are single. ___Their___ gender is female.

4. My name is Livia. ___My___ occupation is nurse. ___I___ am from Colombia.

5. This is my friend, Sarah. ___Her___ birthplace is Canada. ___Her___ telephone number is 555-9876. ___She___ is a student in my class.

Community: School Personnel

A Learn new words.

nurse

librarian

security guard

principal

secretary

B Find and underline the words from Activity A.

Bradley Middle School Personnel Directory

Henry Smith	Principal	Main Office
Susan Berg	Secretary	Main Office
Mary Hunter	Nurse	Room 101
Paul Trent	Security guard	Room 102
Rosa Winn	Librarian	Room 105
Teachers		
Karen Tam	ESL 1	Room 201
Luis Soldan	ESL 2	Room 221
Jack Lee	Math	Room 202
Jack Lee	9th grade	Room 202

C Look at the chart in Activity B. Match the names to the occupations.

1. Luis Soldan
2. Mary Hunter
3. Henry Smith
4. Susan Berg
5. Rosa Winn
6. Paul Trent

a. librarian
b. security guard
c. teacher
d. principal (*pén vó bô*)
e. nurse
f. secretary

D Look at the chart in Activity B. Write the name(s) next to the places.

1. Room 105 — Rosa Winn
2. Room 201 — Karen Tam
3. Room 221 — Luis Soldan
4. Room 101 — Mary Hunter
5. Main Office — Henry Smith, Susan Berg

E **Conversation Challenge.** Read the conversation. Write the room numbers from the directory in Activity B.

A: Hi. Is this Ms. Tam's class?

B: No, this is Mr. Lee's class.

A: **Do you know where*** Ms. Tam's class is?

B: It's in Room _201_.

A: I thought *this* was Room _201_. (*thót*)

B: No. This is Room _202_.

A: Oh. Thanks.

*Useful Expressions

to ask directions

Do you know where …
Where would I find …
How do I get to …

TAKE IT OUTSIDE: INTERVIEW A FAMILY MEMBER, FRIEND, OR CLASSMATE. ASK THE QUESTIONS. WRITE THE ANSWERS.

What is the room number of your class?	What is your teacher's name?	Is there a security guard at your school?

Family: Mailing Letters

Keiko sends the letter.

A Learn new words. Find and underline these words.

send	receive	letter
return address	stamp	envelope

Dear Mrs. Lynch,

    I am a student at Central Community College. I am from Japan. I am also a teacher. I can practice English with your students. I can teach your students to write their names in Japanese. My telephone number is (310) 555-0123.

Sincerely,
Keiko Ishikawa

letter

return address

stamp

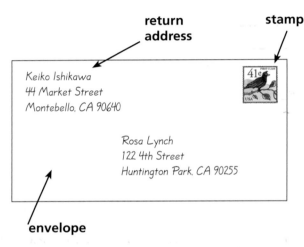

Keiko Ishikawa
44 Market Street
Montebello, CA 90640

Rosa Lynch
122 4th Street
Huntington Park, CA 90255

envelope

Rosa receives the letter.

B Answer the questions.

1. Who writes the letter? _____Keiko_____
2. Who reads the letter? _____Lynch_____
3. What is Keiko's last name? _____Ishikawa_____
4. What is Mrs. Lynch's first name? _____Rosa_____
5. What is Keiko's address? __44 Market Street Montebello, CA 90640__

C Check *yes* or *no* about the letter and the envelope in Activity A.

1. Keiko writes the letter. ☑ yes ☐ no
2. Rosa's address is 44 Market Street. ☐ yes ☑ no
3. Keiko is from Japan. ☑ yes ☐ no
4. Rosa's city is Huntington Park. ☑ yes ☐ no
5. Keiko's last name is Lynch. ☐ yes ☑ no
6. Mrs. Lynch's first name is Rosa. ☑ yes ☐ no

D Write your name and address on the envelope. Write the new words on the lines.

letter   envelope   stamp   return address

Dear Mrs. Lynch,

I am a student. My name is Mark. I am from Colombia. I am a teacher. . . .

stamp

envelope

Rosa Lynch
122 4th Street
Huntington Park, CA 90255

....

TAKE IT OUTSIDE: ASK A FAMILY MEMBER, FRIEND, OR COWORKER FOR HIS OR HER NAME AND ADDRESS. WRITE IT ON THE ENVELOPE. WRITE YOUR NAME AND ADDRESS ON THE ENVELOPE FOR THE RETURN ADDRESS.

13

Practice Test

DIRECTIONS: Answer the questions. Use the Answer Sheet.

1. What is her telephone number?
   A. (617) 555-5643
   B. Martha Hayes
   C. 544 Martindale Street
   D. February 1, 1956

2. What is my address?
   A. (617) 555-5643
   B. 555-89-7723
   C. 544 Martindale Street
   D. February 1, 1956

3. What is Susan's city?
   A. Chicago
   B. Mexico
   C. 22903
   D. 212

4. What is Leo's marital status?
   A. male
   B. single
   C. gender
   D. teacher

5. What is Lana's gender?
   A. married
   B. nurse
   C. address
   D. female

6. What thing opens and closes?
   A. a door
   B. a map
   C. a floor
   D. a partner

7. What do you read?
   A. a window
   B. a book
   C. a teacher
   D. a pen

8. What do you take out?
   A. a word
   B. a hand
   C. a piece of paper
   D. a window

ANSWER SHEET

	A	B	C	D
1	A	B	C	D
2	A	B	C	D
3	A	B	C	D
4	A	B	C	D
5	A	B	C	D
6	A	B	C	D
7	A	B	C	D
8	A	B	C	D
9	A	B	C	D
10	A	B	C	D

DIRECTIONS: Look at the envelope to answer the next 2 questions. Use the Answer Sheet on page 14.

Maurice Nzuzi
1981 Tenth Street
Pomona, CA 91766

Sandra Escobar
1921 Telfair Avenue
Pacoima, CA 91331

9. Who sends the letter?
   A. Sandra Escobar
   B. Tenth Street
   C. Maurice Nzuzi
   D. Pomona, CA

10. Who receives the letter?
   A. Sandra Escobar
   B. Telfair Avenue
   C. Maurice Nzuzi
   D. Pomona, CA

HOW DID YOU DO? Count the number of correct answers on your answer sheet. Record this number in the bar graph on the inside back cover.

Identifying Places in the Community

A Write the words next to the pictures.

| park | gas station | school | supermarket |

1.
school

2.
supermarket

3.
gas station

4.
park

B Complete the sentences.

1. The _____police station_____ is on Main Street.
2. The _____library_____ is on Baxter Street.
3. The _____Community Center_____ is on Elm Street.
4. The _____Fire Station_____ is on Madison Street.
5. The __Cedar Park Elementary school__ is on Cedar Park Street.

G-16

M
O
N
T
E
B
E
L
L
O

Montebello, CITY OF —
Cedar Park Elementary School
   100 Cedar Park Street............. (323) 555-1023
Community Center
   201 Elm Street........................ (323) 555-5289
Fire Station
   1300 Madison Street................ (323) 555-9002
Library
   251 Baxter Street.................... (323) 555-7700
Police Station
   1250 Main Street..................... (323) 555-8990

UNITED STATES GOVERNMENT
Post Office
   1100 State Street..................... (323) 555-4563

C Match the questions and answers. Use the information in Activity B.

Questions	Answers
1. _b_ Where's the post office?	a. It's on Main Street.
2. _a_ Where's the police station?	b. It's on State Street.
3. _e_ Where's the library?	c. It's on Cedar Park Street.
4. _d_ Where's the fire station?	d. It's on Madison Street.
5. _f_ Where's the community center?	e. It's on Baxter Street.
6. _c_ Where's the school?	f. It's on Elm Street.

D Circle the correct answers.

1. Where's the community center?
   (A.) It's on Elizabeth Avenue.   B. Yes, it is.

2. What's the phone number?
   (A.) 555-5289   B. It's on Elm Street.

3. What's the address?
   (A.) 201 Elm Street.   B. Thanks.

4. Thanks.
   A. Yes, it is.   (B.) You're welcome.

queó khun

E Complete the conversations. Use *When, What,* or *Where.*

1. A: ____When____ is your birthday?
   B: On October 10th.

2. A: ____Where____ is the post office?
   B: It's on Madison Street.

3. A: ____What____ is your address?
   B: 2021 Cedar Street, Apartment B.

4. A: ____Where____ are the laundromats in your town?
   B: On Main Street, Center Street, and Oak Street.

5. A: ____What____ is the phone number of the Community Center on Elm Street?
   B: (323) 555-5289.

6. A: ____When____ is your English class?
   B: It's at 9:00.

F Answer the questions about your town or city.

1. Where's your post office?   _It's on Main Street_
2. Where's your fire station?   _It's on Main Street_
3. Where's your library?   _It's on Main Street_
4. Where's your police station?   _____

Giving Directions

A Complete the sentences.

next to	between	in back of
across from	on the corner of	

1. The bank is _____next to_____ the post office.
2. The drugstore is _____across from_____ the police station.
3. The park is _____in back of_____ the hospital.
4. The movie theater is _____between_____ the gas station and the drugstore.
5. The library is _____on the corner of_____ Third Street and State Street.

B Complete the sentences.

EXAMPLE: The _____gas station_____ is across from the library.

1. The fire station is between the post office and the _____post office_____ .
2. The park is in back of the _____hospital_____ .
3. The _____restaurant_____ is next to the school.
4. The gas station is on the corner of _____State Street_____ and _____third Street_____ .
5. The _____gas Station_____ is next to the laundromat.

C Write the answers. Use the information in Activity A.

1. A: Excuse me. Where's the library?
   B: _____The library is on the corner of state street and third street_____
2. A: Excuse me. Where's the fire station?
   B: _____the fire Station is between post office and police station_____
3. A: Excuse me. Where's the drugstore?
   B: _____the drugstore is next to movie theater_____
4. A: Excuse me. Where's the gas station?
   B: _____Gas Station is on the corner of state street and third street_____

D Circle 5 places near or in Ballenbrook Estates.

BALLENBROOK ESTATES

VISIT OUR NEW HOMES
STARTING IN THE 150s

Near excellent (schools,)
supermarkets, and restaurants.
Ballenbrook Estates has its
own community center,
post office, and laundromat.

CALL 555-7892 TODAY.

E Write the places in the correct place in the chart.

NEAR BALLENBROOK ESTATES	IN BALLENBROOK ESTATES
schools	community center
supermarkets	post office
Restaurants	Laundromat

F Answer the questions about you.

1. Who sits in front of you? _____

2. Who sits in back of you? _____

3. Who sits next to you? _____

In Town

A Write the words next to the signs.

| car | pay phone | ATM | police |
| bus stop | mailbox | parking | stoplight |

1. _Parking_

2. _bus stop_

3. _mailbox_

4. _pay phone_

5. _car_

6. _stoplight_

7. _ATM_

8. _police_

B Put the conversation in order. Number the sentences from first (1) to last (4).

_4_ No problem.

_1_ Excuse me. Is there a pay phone around here?

_2_ Yes, there's one on Trade Street. It's in front of the supermarket.

_3_ Thanks a lot.

C Look at the map. Answer the questions. Write *Yes, there is* or *No, there isn't*.

1. Is there a pay phone in the post office?

    No, there isn't

Yes, there is./No, there isn't.

2. Is there parking next to the supermarket?

3. Is there a bus stop on Third Street?

4. Is there an ATM in the library?

5. Is there a pay phone in the drugstore?

6. Is there an ATM in the drugstore?

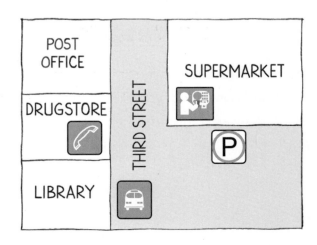

D Match the questions and answers.

Questions

1. _a_ Is there a mailbox near here?
2. _b_ Where's the post office?
3. _d_ What's the phone number?
4. _c_ Next to the library?
5. _e_ Are there any pay phones on this street?

Answers

a. Yes, there are. In front of the bank.
b. It's next to the police station.
c. That's right.
d. It's 555-4092.
e. Yes, there is.

E Look at the map. Write *There is* or *There are* and the number.

1. _____ There is one _____ gas station.
2. _____ There are _____ ATMs.
3. _____ There are _____ pay phones.
4. _____ There is _____ bus stop.
5. _____ There is _____ supermarket.
6. _____ There is _____ mailbox.

> **There is/There are**

COUNTY LIBRARY | ALLSAVE DRUGSTORE | FOODFRESH SUPERMARKET | JIMMIE'S RESTAURANT

MAIL

P

GAS AND GO

F Complete the questions. Write *Is there* or *Are there*. Then answer the questions.

1. A: _____ a movie theater near your home?
   B: _____.

2. A: _____ drugstores in your town?
   B: _____.

3. A: _____ a supermarket near your school?
   B: _____.

4. A: _____ restaurants near your school?
   B: _____.

> **Is there/Are there**
> **Yes, there is.**
> **No, there isn't.**
> **Yes, there are.**
> **No, there aren't.**

21

Reading a U.S. Map

A Circle the correct answer and write the names of the towns on the lines.

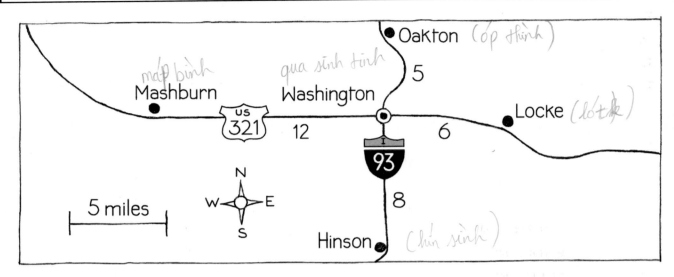

1. _____ is north of Washington.   A. Hinson   (B.) Oakton

2. _____ is west of Washington.   A. Hinson   (B.) Mashburn

3. _____ is south of Washington.   (A.) Hinson   B. Locke

4. Washington is _____ of Locke.   (A.) west   B. south

5. Washington is _____ of Oakton.   A. north   (B.) south

6. Oakton is _____ of Washington.   A. west   (B.) north

B Answer the questions.

1. What town is east of Washington?   _____locke_____

2. What towns are east of Mashburn on Highway 321?   ___washington / locke___

3. What towns are north of Hinson on I-93?   ___washington / oakton___

4. What town is west of Washington?   ___Mashburn___

5. What town is between Hinson and Oakton?   ___washington___

C Complete the sentences. Use the map in Activity A.

1. It is ___5___ miles from Washington to Oakton.
2. Hinson is ___8___ miles from Washington.
3. There are ___12___ miles between Washington and Mashburn.
4. Locke is ___6___ miles from Washington.
5. There are ___5___ miles between Washington and Oakton.
6. There are ___8___ miles between Hinson and Washington.

D Write the math symbols.

+ plus (and)	> is more than	= equals	– minus	< is less than
1 + 2 = 3	6 > 5		3 – 2 = 1	8 < 9

1. How many miles is it from Washington to Oakton and back? 5 + 5 = 10
2. How many miles is it from Oakton to Hinson? 5 + 8 = 13
3. How many miles is it from Mashburn to Locke? 12 + 6 = 18
4. How many miles is it from Washington to Locke and back? 6 __ 6 __ 12
5. Sam's address is 581 Highway 321. It is 2 miles west of Washington, between Washington and Mashburn. How many miles is it from Sam's address to Mashburn? 12 __ 2 __ 10

E Answer the questions about your city or town. Use capitalization and punctuation.

1. How many miles is it from your home to school?
2. What town is north of your city or town?
3. What state do you live in? I live in NJ
4. What state is north of your state?

F Write about you.

I live in the town/city of _____. It is in the state of _____.

The capital of the state is _____. My state is next to _____.

The governor of my state is _____.

Family: Asking for Locations

A Learn new words. Find and circle these words in the map.

gym	cafeteria	main office	nurse's office	playground

HOOVER ELEMENTARY SCHOOL

LIBRARY	106	105		104	103		
CAFETERIA	NURSE'S OFFICE	MAIN OFFICE		101	102	GYM	BUS STOP

not in

← CARS

PLAYGROUND   PARKING LOT

B Complete the sentences.

next to	between	across from	in front of	near

1. The bus stop is _____in front of_____ the gym.
2. Room 102 is _____next to_____ Room 101.
3. The cafeteria is ___in front of / next to___ the library.
4. Room 105 is _____across from_____ the main office.
5. The nurse's office is _____between_____ the cafeteria and the main office.

C Match the questions and answers. Use the map in Activity A.

Questions	Answers
1. _f_ Where's the nurse's office?	a. It's across from the cafeteria.
2. _b_ Where's the library?	b. It's in back of the cafeteria.
3. _e_ Where's the cafeteria?	c. It's across from room 104.
4. _c_ Where's room 101?	d. It's near the gym.
5. _d_ Where's the bus stop?	e. It's next to the nurse's office.
6. _a_ Where's the playground?	f. It's next to the main office.

D Answer the questions. Use the map in Activity A.

1. Where's the bus stop? _It's near the gym._
2. Where's the playground? _It's across from the cafeteria_
3. Where's the nurse's office? _It's next to the main office_
4. Where's the main office? _It's across from room 105._
5. Where's the parking lot? _It's across from the GYM_
6. Where's room 106? _It's next to the library_

E Check *yes* or *no* about the map in Activity A.

1. There is a bus stop. ☑ yes ☐ no
2. The cafeteria is next to the gym. ☐ yes ☑ no
3. There are 6 classrooms. ☑ yes ☐ no
4. The playground is in the school. ☐ yes ☑ no
5. There are 2 libraries. ☐ yes ☑ no

....

TAKE IT OUTSIDE: INTERVIEW A FAMILY MEMBER, FRIEND, OR COWORKER.

What is the name of your child's school? _____

What is the address of your child's school _____

Work: Identifying Forms of Transportation

A Learn new words.

train

airplane

bus

subway

taxi

ferry

B Look at the bus signs. Write the missing information.

> 62   Fifth Ave.

> 14   Market St.

> 72   Community Center

1. A: Can you tell me how to get to the Glendale Community Center?

   B: Sure. Just take Bus ___72 Community Center___. You can get it on the corner of 9th and Broadway.

2. A: Where does the 62 bus go?

   B: Let's see. The 62 bus goes up ___fifth Ave___.

3. A: I need to go to Market Street. Do you know what bus I take?

   B: That's the ___14 Market St___ bus.

C Look at the map.

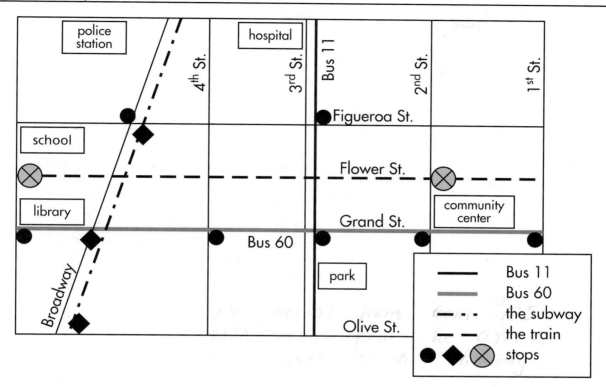

D Write the type of transportation you need.

1. Take ___Bus 11___ to go from the park to the hospital.
2. Take ___the subway___ to go from Grand Street and Broadway to the police station.
3. Take ___the train___ to go from the school to the community center.
4. Take ___bus 60___ to go from the library to the park.
5. Take ___bus 60___ and ___subway___ to go from the community center to the police station.

E **Conversation Challenge. Look at the map. Complete the conversation.**

A: **Excuse me.*** Where's the stop for ___Bus 11?___

B: It's over there, at the corner of <u>Grand</u> Street and <u>3rd</u> Street.

A: It goes to the <u>library</u>, right?

B: Oh, gosh, no. You need ___bus 60___.

A: Oh. Where's the stop?

B: It's near the community center, at ___Grand St___ Street and ___2nd___ Street.

A: Great. Thanks a lot.

B: You're welcome.

*Useful Expressions
to get someone's attention
Excuse me.
Pardon me.
I beg your pardon.

👥 Practice this conversation with a partner.

Practice Test

DIRECTIONS: Look at the map to answer the next 5 questions. Use the Answer Sheet.

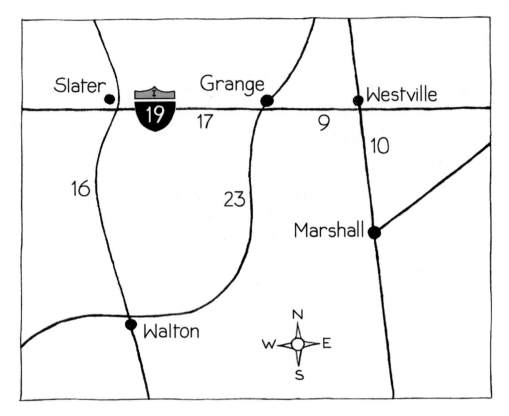

ANSWER SHEET

	A	B	C	D
1	A	B	C	D
2	A	B	C	D
3	A	B	C	D
4	A	B	C	D
5	A	B	C	D
6	A	B	C	D
7	A	B	C	D
8	A	B	C	D
9	A	B	C	D
10	A	B	C	D

1. How far is it from Walton to Grange?

   A. 17 miles   B. 9 miles   C. 23 miles   D. 32 miles

2. How far is it from Slater to Grange?

   A. 17 miles   B. 34 miles   C. 26 miles   D. 32 miles

3. What direction is Westville from Marshall?

   A. north   B. west   C. south   D. east

4. What city is west of Grange on I-19?

   A. Slater   B. Walton   C. Westville   D. Marshall

5. What city is east of Grange on I-19?

   A. Slater   B. Walton   C. Westville   D. Marshall

DIRECTIONS: Look at the map to answer the next 5 questions. Use the Answer Sheet on page 28.

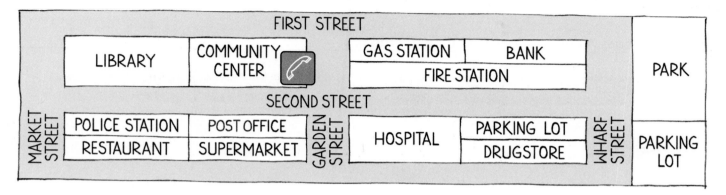

6. Where is the bank?
    A. It's on First Street.
    B. It's on Market Street.
    C. It's on Garden Street.
    D. It's on Second Street.

7. Where is the supermarket?
    A. It's next to the bank.
    B. It's next to the library.
    C. It's next to the restaurant.
    D. It's next to the hospital.

8. Where is the fire station?
    A. It's on First Street.
    B. It's across from the hospital.
    C. It's next to the drugstore.
    D. It's between the gas station and the bank.

9. Which sentence is correct?
    A. The community center is across from the library.
    B. There are 3 parking lots.
    C. There are 2 restaurants.
    D. The post office is on the corner of Second Street and Garden Street.

10. Where is a pay phone?
    A. It's in the police station.
    B. It's in the parking lot next to the park.
    C. It's in the community center.
    D. It's in back of the hospital.

HOW DID YOU DO? Count the number of correct answers on your answer sheet. Record this number in the bar graph on the inside back cover.

Spotlight: Writing

A Read stories A and B below. Find these words.

Find the words with C.
c _a_ _r_ _o_ _l_
C __ __ __ __ __ __ __
c __ __
c __ __ __ __ __

Find the words with R.
r _e_ _a_ _d_
R __ __ __
r __ __ __ __ __
r __ __ __ __

STORIES

A.

Hi! My name is Carol. I'm from Colorado. I like to read, talk on the telephone, and go to the movies. I don't like to watch TV.

B.

My name is David. I'm from Reno, Nevada. I like to drive my car, listen to the radio, and go to parties. I don't like to clean my room.

B Correct the story. Add 5 punctuation marks.

My name is Ann I like to watch

TV read books and go to school I don't

like to go to the supermarket

> **FOCUS ON WRITING: Punctuation Marks**
>
> • Use a period (.) at the end of a sentence.
>   *Example*: He's a doctor.
> • Use a comma (,) between words in a series.
>   *Example*: I like to read, go to the library, and go to the park.

C Complete the chart about you. Use the words below. Then add 3 more activities.

dance

I like to	*I don't like to*
dance	

go to the dentist

relax

eat

wash dishes

D Write your own story.

My name is _____

_____

_____

_____

_____

> *Add your picture here.*

31

Telling Time

A Write the times below the clocks.

1. __2:00__   2. __8:10__   3. __9:45__   4. __10:15__   5. __11:00__

6. __4:30__   7. __1:45__   8. __7:30__   9. __15:15__   10. __6:20__

B Write the numbers another way.

EXAMPLES: 45 __forty-five__   __12__ twelve

1. 15 __fifteen__   6. __33__ thirty-three

2. __46__ forty-six   7. 52 __fivety – two__

3. 17 __seventeen__   8. 35 __thirty – five__

4. 32 __thirty – two__   9. __55__ fifty-five

5. __29__ twenty-nine   10. 18 __eighteen__

C Answer the questions. Use the clocks below.

EXAMPLES: A: What time is it?   B: It's three-thirty.

1. A: Excuse me. What time is it?   B: __It's one o'clock__.

2. A: Excuse me. What time is it?   B: __It's nine – thirty__.

3. A: Excuse me. What time is it?   B: __It's ten o'clock__.

4. A: Excuse me. What time is it?   B: __It's seven – thirty__.

D Complete the sentences.

in the morning	at night	analog	noon	after
in the afternoon	A.M.	P.M.	in the evening	digital

1. 8:00 A.M. is eight o'clock _in the morning_.
2. Another way to say *after noon* is _P.M._.
3. Another name for 12:00 P.M. is _noon_.
4. Another way to say *in the morning* is _AM_.
5. The number 15 is _after_ 14.
6. Another way to say *6:00 P.M.* is six o'clock _in the evening_.
7. Another way to say *10:00 P.M.* is ten o'clock _at night_.
8. **4:30** This clock is a _digital_ clock.
9. This clock is an _analog_ clock.
10. Another way to say *3:00 P.M.* is three o'clock _in the afternoon_.

E Complete the questions. Write *is* or *are*.

is   are

1. When _is_ your bank open?
2. When _is_ your class?
3. When _are_ drugstores open?
4. When _are_ supermarkets open?
5. When _is_ your library open?

F Answer the questions in Activity E.

1. _____
2. _____
3. _____
4. _____
5. _____

At the Library

A Find these words in the puzzle. Circle them.

morning	night
Monday	time
Thursday	computer
telephone	pen
afternoon	checkout
week	video
closed	clock
forty	desk
library	from
Wednesday	five

```
m o r n i n g u p f a M
t e l e p h o n e r d o
a f t e r n o o n o b n
b v q n i g h t i m e d
l c o m p u t e r s p a
e l u x w l i b r a r y
f o r v i d e o f i v e
o c y o u d o o r j i n
r k i c h e c k o u t z
t T h u r s d a y z i p
y s w e e k c l o s e d
W e d n e s d a y g o t
```

B Complete the sentences. Use words from the puzzle.

EXAMPLE: This unit is about __time__ and money.

1. _____Wednesday_____ is the day after Tuesday.

2. The day before Friday is _____Thursday_____.

3. The day after Sunday is _____Monday_____.

4. The library is open from ten o'clock in the _____morning_____ to nine o'clock at _____night_____ on Wednesday.

5. On Sundays and Thursdays the library is not open. It is _____closed_____.

C Look at the hours of the post office. Answer the questions.

> **U.S. Post Office**
> **Hours of Operation**
>
> Sunday: CLOSED
> Monday: from 7:00 A.M. to 5:30 P.M.
> Tuesday: from 7:00 A.M. to 5:30 P.M.
> Wednesday: from 7:00 A.M. to 5:30 P.M.
> Thursday: from 7:00 A.M. to 5:30 P.M.
> Friday: from 7:00 A.M. to 4:30 P.M.
> Saturday: from 8:00 A.M. to noon

1. When is the post office open on Monday? _From 7:00 A.M. to 5:30 P.M._
2. Is the post office open on Saturday? _From 8:00 AM to noon_
3. Is the post office open on Sunday? _____
4. When is the post office open on Friday? _____
5. When is the post office open on Thursday? _____
6. When is the post office open on Tuesday? _____

D Circle *yes* or *no* for each sentence.

1. The post office is open on Wednesday at noon.   (yes)   no
2. The post office is closed on Saturday at 6:00 P.M.   (yes)   no
3. The post office is open on Tuesday at midnight.   yes   (no)
4. The post office is closed on Sunday.   (yes)   no
5. The post office is open on Friday at 2:00 P.M.   (yes)   (no)

E Write the words in the correct order.

1. the library / When is / on Tuesday / open

   When is the library open on Tuesday?

2. the supermarket / open / at midnight / Is

   The supermarket is open at midnight?

3. is / at 5:00 A.M. / closed / The gas station

   The gas station is closed at 5:00 AM.

4. The hospital / Sunday to Saturday / is open

   The hospital is open Sunday to Saturday.

5. is closed / at 6:00 P.M. / The park

   The park is closed at 6:00 PM.

Counting Money

A Put the words in order.

> < is less than   > is more than   = equals

> dime   dollar   nickel   quarter   penny

1. ___penny___ < 2. ___nickle___ < 3. ___dime___ < 4. ___quarter___ < 5. ___dollar___

B Write the amounts another way.

EXAMPLE: a penny ___1¢___   a nickel ___5¢___

1. a quarter ___25¢___
2. a dollar ___$1.00___
3. ___5 dollars___ $5.00
4. a dime ___10¢___
5. twenty dollars ___$20___
6. ___fifty dollars___ $50.00
7. ___a dime___ 10¢
8. one thousand dollars ___$1000___

C Answer the questions.

EXAMPLE: How much is 20¢ and 30¢? ___50¢___

1. How much is one dollar and 10 dollars? ___$110___
2. How much is a quarter and a nickel? ___30¢___
3. How much is 50 dollars and 3 dollars? ___$53.00___
4. How much is a dime and a quarter? ___35¢___
5. How much is 25¢ and 40¢? ___65¢___
6. How much is it? ___71¢___
7. How much is it? ___20¢___
8. How much is it? ___65¢___
9. How much is a penny and a nickel? ___6¢___
10. How much is 10¢ and a nickel? ___15¢___

> How much?

6.

7.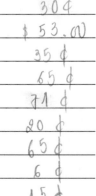

8.

D Read the sign. Match the questions and answers.

Movie Town DVDs

New DVDs
$4.50
each for
2 evenings

Regular DVDs
$3.95
for 5 evenings
or 3 for $10

Video Games
$2.95
for 5
evenings

Questions	Answers
1. How much is a new DVD? _b_	a. No, it's not. It's $10 for 3 DVDs
2. How much is a video game? _e_	b. It's $4.50 for 2 evenings.
3. How much is a regular DVD? _c_	c. It's $3.95 for 5 evenings.
4. Is a new DVD $4.50 for 3 evenings? _d_	d. No, it's not. It's $4.50 for 2 evenings.
5. Is a regular DVD $10 for one DVD? _a_	e. It's $2.95 for 5 evenings.

E Answer the questions.

1. How much is a DVD at your video store? _____

2. How much is an overdue book at your library? _____

3. How much is this workbook? _____

4. How much is a DVD at your library? _____

5. How much is a DVD on the Internet? _____

Reading and Writing Checks

A Read the checks. Circle *yes* or *no*.

SUSAN KELLER
121 Beacon St.
Van Nuys, CA 91406
072
DATE 3/12/12
PAY TO THE ORDER OF Movie Town DVDs $ 7.90
Seven and 90/100 DOLLARS
TRUE BANK
California
MEMO DVDs and games
Susan Keller
⑆012345678⑆: 123⑈456 7⑈ 0072

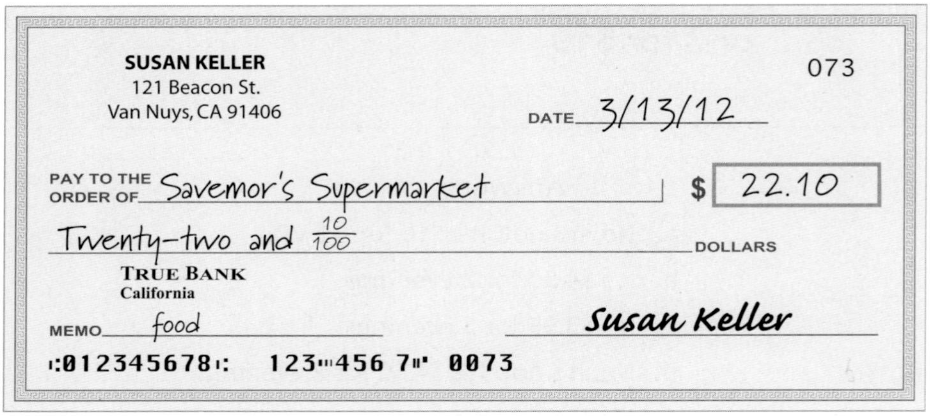
SUSAN KELLER
121 Beacon St.
Van Nuys, CA 91406
073
DATE 3/13/12
PAY TO THE ORDER OF Savemor's Supermarket $ 22.10
Twenty-two and 10/100 DOLLARS
TRUE BANK
California
MEMO food
Susan Keller
⑆012345678⑆: 123⑈456 7⑈ 0073

1. The check to Movie Town DVDs is for $22.10. yes (no)
2. The check to Movie Town DVDs is number 072. yes no
3. Susan Keller writes the checks. yes no
4. The check for $22.10 is check number 073. yes no
5. The check for $7.90 is for DVDs and games. yes no
6. Susan writes a check to FoodFresh Supermarket. yes no
7. Susan writes a check to Movie Town DVDs in February. yes no
8. Susan lives in True Bank, California. yes no
9. Susan's zip code is 31305. yes no
10. Susan writes a check to Savemor's Supermarket on March 13. yes no

B Circle the correct answers.

1. What is the name of the supermarket?

   A. Savemor's   B. Susan Keller

2. How much is check number 072 for?

   A. $7.90   B. $22.10

3. What is check number 073 for?

   A. videos   B. food

4. What is Susan Keller's address?

   A. 121 Beacon St.   B. True Bank, California

5. What is the amount of the check to Movie Town DVDs?

   A. DVDs and games   B. $7.90

C Write the missing numbers.

1. $10.00 + $3.50 = _____

2. $4.95 + $2.95 = _____

3. $22.10 + $7.90 = _____

4. $4.00 + 95¢ = _____

5. $12.00 + $2.95 = _____

6. $10.00 – $5.00 = _____

7. $5.00 – $.50 = _____

8. $1.00 – 25¢ = _____

9. $50.00 – $7.00 = _____

10. $20.00 – $12.00 = _____

D Read the chart. Write the missing numbers.

CHECK #	TO	AMOUNT	FOR	BALANCE
072	Movie Town DVDs	$7.90	DVDs	$100.00
				– $ 7.90
073	Savemor's Supermarket	$22.10	food	= $ 92.10
				– $ 22.10
074	Jiffy Gas	$20.00	gas	= $ 70.00
				– $ 20.00
075	Post Office	$10.00	stamps	=
				– $ 10.00
076	Safe Drugstore	$15.00	drugs	= $ 40.00
077	Movie Theater	$15.00	tickets	

Work: Time Cards

A Look at the time card below. Write the number of hours in the TOTAL HOURS column.

Regular Hours < or = 40 hours in a week   Overtime > 40 hours in a week

TIME CARD

DATE 10/15/12	
EMPLOYEE'S NAME Martin Ruiz	**SOC.SEC.NO.** 555-00-5555

ADDRESS
1534 Green Street, Richmond, VA

POSITION Machinist	**DEPT.** Printing	**EMPLOYEE NO.** B915

NAME OF EMPLOYER
Southside Distributors

	A.M.		P.M.		OVERTIME		TOTAL HOURS	
	IN	OUT	IN	OUT	IN	OUT	REGULAR	OVERTIME
MONDAY	8:00	11:30	12:30	5:00			8:00	0
TUESDAY	7:30	11:30	1:00	5:00				
WEDNESDAY	7:30	12:00	1:00	5:00				
THURSDAY	8:00	12:00	1:00	4:30				
FRIDAY	8:00	11:30	12:30	5:00				
SATURDAY					9:00	1:00		4
SUNDAY							0	
						WEEKLY TOTAL		

SIGNATURE: *Martin Ruiz*

B Look at the time card. Complete the sentences.

1. Martin's occupation is _____.

2. Martin's last name is _____.

3. Martin's employer is _____.

4. His address is _____.

5. His job is from _____ to _____ on Monday and Friday.

C Read the information for Lily Jen. Write the times on the time card.

Lily Jen is a cashier at Ray's Supermarket. Her address is 32 Market Street, Rockford, IL. Her employee number is 302B-9. Lily works three days a week. Her hours on Monday are 10 A.M. to 4 P.M. On Wednesday, Lily's hours are 8 A.M. to noon. On Friday, her hours are 1 P.M. to 8 P.M.

TIME CARD

DATE							
EMPLOYEE'S NAME				SOC.SEC.NO. 987-00-6543			
ADDRESS							
POSITION	DEPT. Checkout			EMPLOYEE NO.			
NAME OF EMPLOYER							

	A.M.		P.M.		OVERTIME		TOTAL HOURS	
	IN	OUT	IN	OUT	IN	OUT	REGULAR	OVERTIME
MONDAY								
TUESDAY								
WEDNESDAY								
THURSDAY								
FRIDAY								
SATURDAY								
SUNDAY								
						WEEKLY TOTAL		

D Read the conversation below. Complete the sentences.

A: Hello. This is <u>Tom Parkman</u>.

B: Hi, <u>Mr. Parkman</u>. This is <u>Nestor Ruiz</u>. I'm going to be a little late today.

A: What's the matter?

B: The bus is late.

A: What time will you be here?

B: By <u>10 A.M.</u>

A: See you then.

👥 Now practice the conversation with a partner. Use different names and times.

Community: Methods of Payment

A Learn new words. Look at the pictures. Write the words under the picture.

Methods of Payment

cash   credit card   check   debit card

1. _____

2. _____

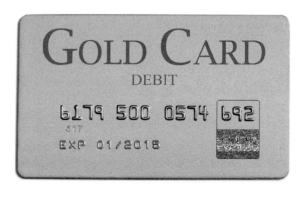

3. _____

4. _____

B Look at the expenses below. Write the methods of payment you use (cash, check, credit card, debit card).

1. pay phone   _____
2. a magazine   _____
3. gas   _____
4. parking   _____
5. a pen   _____
6. the bus   _____
7. a computer   _____
8. laundromat   _____

C Look at the pictures. Complete the conversations. Use your own ideas for method of payment.

1. A: How much is this _____?
   B: $299. How do you want to pay?
   A: With _____.

2. A: How much is this _____?
   B: $1.99. How do you want to pay?
   A: With _____.

3. A: How much is this _____?
   B: $16.99. How do you want to pay?
   A: With _____.

4. A: How much are the _____?
   B: $9.62. How do you want to pay?
   A: With _____.

Practice the conversations with a partner.

TAKE IT OUTSIDE: INTERVIEW A FAMILY MEMBER, FRIEND, OR COWORKER.

Things you buy	Method of payment
Food	Debit card

Practice Test

DIRECTIONS: Answer the questions. Use the Answer Sheet.

1. It's one o'clock.

   A.

   B.

   C.

   D.

2. It's 3:30.

   A.

   B.

   C.

   D.

3. It's 20¢.

   A. two dimes
   B. two nickels
   C. a dime and a nickel
   D. a nickel and a penny

4. How much money is it?
   A. $8.00
   B. $.80
   C. 8¢
   D. $.08

ANSWER SHEET
1 Ⓐ Ⓑ Ⓒ Ⓓ
2 Ⓐ Ⓑ Ⓒ Ⓓ
3 Ⓐ Ⓑ Ⓒ Ⓓ
4 Ⓐ Ⓑ Ⓒ Ⓓ
5 Ⓐ Ⓑ Ⓒ Ⓓ
6 Ⓐ Ⓑ Ⓒ Ⓓ
7 Ⓐ Ⓑ Ⓒ Ⓓ
8 Ⓐ Ⓑ Ⓒ Ⓓ
9 Ⓐ Ⓑ Ⓒ Ⓓ
10 Ⓐ Ⓑ Ⓒ Ⓓ

5. How much is two dimes and two dollars?
   A. $2.10   B. $20.10   C. $2.02   D. $2.20

6. How much is five nickels and five dollars?
   A. $25.25   B. $5.05   C. $25.05   D. $5.25

7. How much is the stamp?

   A.

   B.

   C.

   D.

DIRECTIONS: Thomas Kennedy writes a check to Newtown Drugs for $24.50 on 9/17/12. Look at the check to answer the next 3 questions. Use the Answer Sheet on page 44.

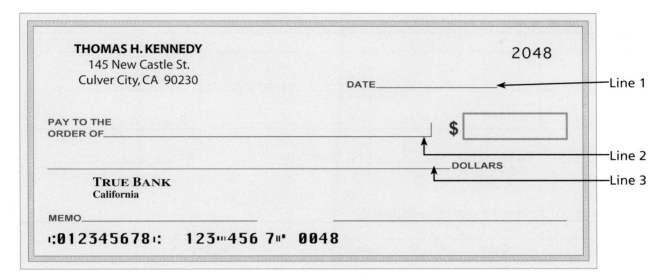

8. What is on Line 3?
   A. 9/17/12
   B. Newtown Drugs
   C. Twenty-four and 50/100
   D. Medicine; Thomas Kennedy

9. What is on Line 1?
   A. 9/17/12
   B. Newtown Drugs; $24.50
   C. Twenty-four and 50/100
   D. Medicine; Thomas Kennedy

10. What is on Line 2?
    A. 9/17/12
    B. Newton Drugs; $24.50
    C. Twenty-four and 50/100
    D. Medicine; Thomas Kennedy

HOW DID YOU DO? Count the number of correct answers on your answer sheet. Record this number in the bar graph on the inside back cover.

Identifying Months

A Write the missing months.

1. January	2. _____	3. _____	4. April
5. _____	6. June	7. _____	8. _____
9. _____	10. _____	11. November	12. _____

B Write the names of 2 months under each word.

Hot	Cold	Rainy	Sunny
July		*April*	
_____	_____	_____	_____
_____	_____	_____	_____

C Look at the graph. Write the number of birthdays for each month.

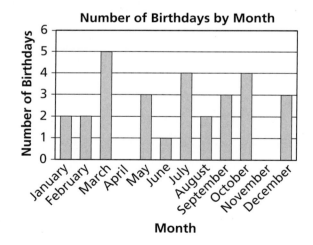

Number of Birthdays by Month

1. February _____2_____

2. March _____

3. April _____

4. July _____

5. November _____

6. December _____

D Circle the correct answers.

1. There are _____ days in a week.

   Ⓐ seven   B. four   C. twenty-four

2. There are _____ days in the month of July.

   A. twenty-four   B. twenty-eight   C. thirty-one

3. There are _____ days in the month of April.

   A. seven   B. thirty   C. twenty-eight

4. There are _____ hours in a day.

   A. thirty   B. twenty-eight   C. twenty-four

5. There are _____ months in a year.

   A. 24   B. 12   C. 7

6. There are _____ minutes in an hour.

   A. 30   B. 60   C. 100

E Complete the survey.

LOS ANGELES COUNTY ADULT SCHOOL SURVEY

Complete the survey with the correct information.

1. There are _____ students in my class.

2. There are _____ classes in a week.

3. What time is the class?   _____

4. What is your teacher's name?   _____

Circle the days of the class.
Mon.   Tues.   Wed.   Thurs.   Fri.   Sat.   Sun.

Circle the months of the class.
January   February   March   April   May   June   July   August   September   October   November   December

---

Events on a Calendar

A Write the words next to the pictures.

> doctor's appointment   PTA meeting   job interview
> dental appointment   basketball game   birthday party

1.  _____

2.  _____

3. _____

4.  _____

5.  _____

6. _____

B Write the ordinal numbers.

EXAMPLE: ten → _____tenth_____

1. one → _____

2. seven → _____

3. fifteen → _____

4. three → _____

5. nine → _____

6. 8 → _____

7. 13 → _____

8. 2 → _____

9. 5 → _____

10. 12 → _____

C Put the conversation in order. Number the sentences from first (1) to last (5).

_____ What day is that?

_____ Oh, sorry. I have a job interview on Thursday.

_____ It's Thursday.

__1__ Do you want to meet on the 2nd?

_____ Some other time, then.

D Look at Marta's calendar. Match the questions and answers.

SUN.	MON.	TUES.	WED.	THURS.	FRI.	SAT.
	1	2 7:30 P.M. PTA meeting	3	4	5 8:00 P.M. basketball game	6 2:00 P.M. Tom's birthday party
7	8 9:00 A.M. job interview	9	10 1:30 P.M. dentist	11	12 3:30 P.M. Dr. Ling	13

Questions

1. When is Marta's job interview?
2. What day is Marta's dental appointment?
3. What date is the birthday party?
4. What time is the PTA meeting?
5. What day is Marta's appointment with Dr. Ling?
6. What time is the basketball game?

Answers

a. It's at 7:30 P.M.
b. It's at 9:00 A.M. on the 8th.
c. It's the 6th.
d. It's on Friday the 12th.
e. It's Wednesday the 10th.
f. It's at 8:00 P.M.

E Complete the sentences about Marta's calendar.

1. _____Marta's job interview_____ is at 9:00AM.

2. _____ is on Saturday the 6th at 2:00PM.

3. _____ is on Wednesday at 1:30 P.M.

4. _____ is on Friday at 8:00 P.M.

F Answer the questions about you.

1. Do you have a job interview? When? _____

2. When is your birthday? _____

3. What appointments are on your calendar? _____

49

Unit 4: Calendars

Keeping Track of Appointments

A Write the numbers another way.

EXAMPLE: __4th__ = fourth

1. _____ = seventeenth

2. 22nd = _____

3. 20th = _____

4. _____ = twenty-third

5. 28th = _____

B Look at the card. Answer the questions.

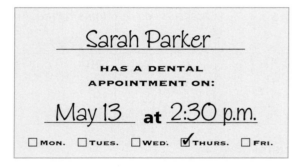

__Sarah Parker__

HAS A DENTAL APPOINTMENT ON:

__May 13__ **at** __2:30 p.m.__

☐ MON. ☐ TUES. ☐ WED. ☑ THURS. ☐ FRI.

1. What day of the week is the appointment?

   _____

2. What time is it?

   _____

3. Who is the appointment for?

   _____

4. What date is it?

   _____

C Circle the correct answers.

EXAMPLE: His appointment is on the _____.

(A.) 8th   B. 8

1. There are _____ students in my class.

   A. 25   B. 25th

2. I have a meeting on the _____.

   A. five   B. fifth

3. There is a game on the _____ of March.

   A. 21st   B. 21

4. Her birthday is the _____ of February.

   A. one   B. first

5. December is the _____ month.

   A. twelfth   B. 12

6. There are _____ Mondays in July.

   A. fourth   B. four

D Write the dates another way.

1. 2/9/11 = _____

2. 7/15/99 = _____

3. August 1, 2002 = _____

4. 5/31/1960 = _____

5. March 3, 1991 = _____

6. 01/01/13 = _____

7. April 9, 2001 = _____

8. 12/25/72 = _____

9. 9/12/10 = _____

10. June 8, 1995 = _____

E Write the words in the correct order. Write questions and answers.

EXAMPLE: A: What / doctor's appointment / is / your / time

_____*What time is your doctor's appointment*_____?

B: at / It's / 3:00 P.M.

_____.

1. A: the basketball game / is / What day

_____?

B: on Friday / It's

_____.

2. A: the PTA meeting / is / When

_____?

B: It's / 13th / March / on

_____.

3. A: is that / day / What

_____?

B: Tuesday / It's

_____.

F Complete the sentences with *in, at,* or *on*.

1. The party is _____*on*_____ Saturday.

2. The English class begins at 8:00 _____*at*_____ night.

3. My wife's birthday is _____*in*_____ September.

4. The appointment is _____*on*_____ August 29th.

5. Naida's class is _____*in*_____ the winter.

6. The library is closed _____*on*_____ Tuesdays.

Identifying Holidays

A Complete the sentences.

ACROSS

1. The holiday on February 14th is _____ Day.

3. July 4th is _____ Day.

4. _____ is on the fourth Thursday in November.

6. The first day of January is _____ Day.

DOWN

2. _____ is the first Tuesday after the first Monday in November.

5. Labor _____ is on the first Monday in September.

B Write the words from Activity A in the crossword puzzle below.

C Write the holidays in order.

New Year's Day	Labor Day	Election Day
Valentine's Day	Thanksgiving	Independence Day

1. First: _____ New Year's Day _____

2. Second: _____

3. Third: _____

4. Fourth: _____

5. Fifth: _____

6. Sixth: _____

D Write the words in the correct place in the chart

~~big~~	desk	fun	rainy	student	~~book~~	word	city
new	holiday	old	good	sunny	day	weather	

Adjective   Noun

Adjective	Noun
big	book

E Write sentences about the pictures. Use the adjectives and nouns in Activity D.

1.  _____

2.  _____

3.  _____

Work: Understanding Schedules

A Read the sentences. Look at Miriam's work schedule at Park Drugstore. Answer the questions.

1. Miriam's hours on Sunday are from ___8:00 A.M.___ to ___2:00 P.M.___ .

2. Her hours on Wednesday are from _____ to _____.

3. Her hours on Saturday are from _____ to _____.

4. Miriam is off on _____ and _____.

5. Miriam is at work only 4 hours on _____.

MIRIAM'S SCHEDULE						
Sunday	Monday	Tuesday	Wednesday	Thursday	Friday	Saturday
		off			off	

B Write the number of hours Miriam is at work on each day.

1. Sunday ___6___

2. Monday _____

3. Tuesday _____

4. Wednesday _____

5. Thursday _____

6. Friday _____

7. Saturday _____

C Read Max's hours. Then fill in his schedule. Color the rectangles.

Monday	off	Friday	8–5
Tuesday	9–3	Saturday	10–4
Wednesday	11–5	Sunday	2–6
Thursday	1–6		

MAX'S SCHEDULE

	Sunday	Monday	Tuesday	Wednesday	Thursday	Friday	Saturday
7 A.M.							
8							
9							
10							
11							
12 P.M.							
1							
2							
3							
4							
5							
6							

D **Conversation Challenge.** Read the conversation between Max and Miriam. Miriam is at work. She is calling Max on his cell phone. Complete the sentences.

Max: Hello?

Miriam: Hello, Max? This is Miriam from the drugstore. Where are you? You're late.

Max: I'm off today, right? It's _____.

Miriam: No, it isn't. It's <u>Sunday.</u>

Max: It is? What are my hours today?

Miriam: You work from _____ to _____ today.

Max: OK. But it's only <u>1:00</u>

Miriam: Wrong again. Your watch is one hour slow. It's _____. I'm supposed to be off at <u>2:00</u>. My shift is over.

Max: Oh, no! My watch is broken! I'm sorry! **I'm on my way***!

*Useful Expressions

to say you are coming

I'm on my way.

I'll be right there.

See you soon.

👥 Practice this conversation with a partner. Use your name.

55

Community: Reading Temperatures

A Look at the illustration and read the information. Complete the sentences with words from the box.

1. The 2 temperature scales are _____ and Celsius.

2. In the _____, people use Fahrenheit.

3. Other countries use the _____ scale.

4. Temperatures more than 100°F are very _____.

5. It is very _____ when temperatures are less than 0°C.

> There are 2 temperature scales: Celsius (C) and Fahrenheit (F). People in the United States use the Fahrenheit scale. Other countries use the Celsius temperature scale. Temperatures less than 0 degrees Celsius (0°C) or less than 32 degrees Fahrenheit (32°F) are very cold. Temperatures more than 37°C or 100°F are very hot. Temperatures between 40°F and 60°F are cool.

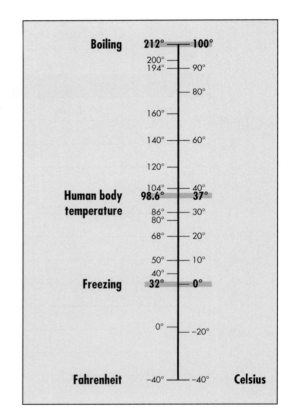

	Fahrenheit	Celsius
Boiling	212°	100°
	200°	
	194°	90°
		80°
	160°	
	140°	60°
	120°	
Human body temperature	104°	40°
	98.6°	37°
	86°	30°
	80°	
	68°	20°
	50°	10°
	40°	
Freezing	32°	0°
	0°	−20°
Fahrenheit	−40°	−40° Celsius

B Read about the weather in 4 cities. Circle the words.

1. In Chihuahua, Mexico, the January temperature is usually between 40°F and 50°F. It is:

   A. cool   B. warm   C. hot

2. On New Year's Day in Sydney, Australia, the temperature is usually between 60°F at night and 80°F during the day. It is:

   A. cool   B. cold   C. warm

3. In Chicago, Illinois, the July temperatures are sometimes above 100°F. It is:

   A. cold   B. hot   C. warm

4. In Moscow, Russia, temperatures in January are less than 20°F. It is:

   A. cold   B. cool   C. warm

C Look at the illustration in Activity A. Fill in the blanks.

1. 10°C = _____°F
2. 104°F = _____°C
3. 86°F = _____°C

4. 20°C = _____°F
5. 194°F = _____°C
6. 0°C = _____°F

D Complete the chart. Add information about your city and another city you know.

City, Country	Season	Temperature
Santiago, Chile	Winter	20° Fahrenheit
Los Angeles, USA	Summer	30° Celsius
Your city: _____	_____	_____
Another city: _____	_____	_____

E **Conversation Challenge.** Read the conversation.

A: Wow! Look at the newspaper. It's <u>cold in Chile</u> right now.

B: What's the temperature?

A: About <u>20°</u>. [Say "degrees" when you see this symbol.]

B: That's not <u>cold</u>—that's <u>warm</u>.

A: **Are you kidding?*** It's <u>winter in Chile</u>.

B: Hm. Is it <u>20° Fahrenheit</u> or <u>20° Celsius</u>?

A: <u>20° Fahrenheit</u>.

B: Oh, you're right. That *is* <u>cold</u>.

> ***Useful Expressions**
>
> *to show surprise*
> Are you kidding?
> You're kidding!
> What?

Practice this conversation with a partner. Use the information in the chart in Activity D and the Useful Expressions box to talk about other cities.

Practice Test

DIRECTIONS: Answer the questions. Circle the correct letter. Use the Answer Sheet.

1. Your appointment is on Friday.

A.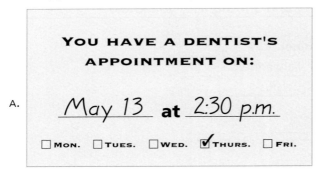

YOU HAVE A DENTIST'S APPOINTMENT ON:

May 13 at 2:30 p.m.

☐ MON. ☐ TUES. ☐ WED. ☑ THURS. ☐ FRI.

B.

Your next appointment is

Aug. 22

10:45 a.m.

M T W TH (F)

C.

Next Appointment

(Mon.) Tues. Wed. Thurs. Fri.

2:30 p.m.

April 15, 2011

D.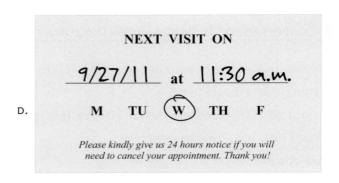

NEXT VISIT ON

9/27/11 at 11:30 a.m.

M TU (W) TH F

Please kindly give us 24 hours notice if you will need to cancel your appointment. Thank you!

2. It's on Tuesday.

A.

M T W T̶H̶ F

B. ☐ MON. ☑ TUES. ☐ WED. ☐ THURS. ☐ FRI.

C.  M̶ TU W TH F

D. Mon. Tues. Wed. Thurs. (Fri.)

3. It's January twenty-fifth.

   A. 25/01/11   B. 2/25/11

   C. 1/25/11   D. 01/08/25

4. His birth date is 04/12/62.

   A. December 4, 1962   B. April 12, 2004

   C. April 12, 1962   D. December 12, 2004

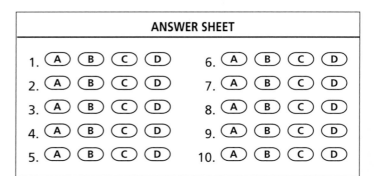

ANSWER SHEET

1. (A) (B) (C) (D)   6. (A) (B) (C) (D)
2. (A) (B) (C) (D)   7. (A) (B) (C) (D)
3. (A) (B) (C) (D)   8. (A) (B) (C) (D)
4. (A) (B) (C) (D)   9. (A) (B) (C) (D)
5. (A) (B) (C) (D)   10. (A) (B) (C) (D)

5. What month is it?

   A. Wednesday   B. August

   C. 1978   D. 6:15 P.M.

DIRECTIONS: Look at the calendar to answer the next 5 questions. Use the Answer Sheet on page 58.

JULY						
SUN.	MON.	TUES.	WED.	THURS.	FRI.	SAT.
		1	2	3	4	5
6	7	8	9	10	11	12
13	14	15	16	17	18	19
20	21	22	23	24	25	26
27	28	29	30	31		

6. July begins on what day of the week?

   A. Monday   B. Tuesday

   C. Wednesday   D. Thursday

7. What day of the week is July 31st?

   A. Monday   B. Tuesday

   C. Wednesday   D. Thursday

8. You have a dental appointment on July 15. What day is it?

   A. Monday   B. Tuesday

   C. Wednesday   D. Thursday

9. Sandy has a job interview on the 23rd. What day is it?

   A. Monday   B. Tuesday

   C. Wednesday   D. Thursday

10. It is the second Friday in July. What is the date?

   A. 7/3/12   B. 7/2/12

   C. 7/11/12   D. 11/7/12

HOW DID YOU DO? Count the number of correct answers on your answer sheet. Record this number in the bar graph on the inside back cover.

Spotlight: Writing

A Read stories A and B. Find these words.

Find the singular nouns with these letters.
h _o_ _l_ _i_ _d_ _a_ _y_
m __ __ __ __ __
f __ __ __ __ __ __
f __ __ __ __ __
d __ __ __ __ __

Find the plural nouns.
__ __ __ __ __ __ __ s
__ __ __ __ __ __ __ __ __ s

STORIES

A.

My name is Ling. My favorite holiday is Chinese New Year. It's in January or February. I like this holiday because I get money from my mother and father. We go to see the parades. We eat a lot of food, too.

B.

My name is Eduardo. My favorite holiday is Independence Day. It's in July. I like this holiday because I am with my family. We eat dinner together. We watch the fireworks at night.

B Correct the punctuation. Add 10 capital letters.

my name is fiona. my favorite holiday
is thanksgiving it is in november i like
this holiday because i visit my family.
we go to california to see them.

FOCUS ON WRITING: Capital Letters

Capitalize:

- the first word in a sentence.
  EXAMPLE: He is a doctor.
- a person's first and last name.
  EXAMPLE: John Smith
- the name of a country, state, or city.
  EXAMPLE: Mexico, California, Los Angeles
- the name of a language.
  EXAMPLE: English, Spanish, Chinese
- the days of the week.
  EXAMPLE: Monday
- the months of the year.
  EXAMPLE: January
- the name of a holiday.
  EXAMPLE: Thanksgiving
- the pronoun *I*.
  EXAMPLE: This is where I live.

C Write your own story.

Add your picture here.

My name is _____

_____

_____

_____

_____

_____

_____

_____

Identifying Clothes and Colors

A Write the words in the correct place in the chart.

necktie	shirt	pants
undershirt	sweater	shorts
briefs	hat	skirt
shoes	T-shirt	dress
boots	jacket	
coat	socks	

SINGULAR	PLURAL
necktie	socks

B Complete the sentences. Write *is* or *are*.

1. What color _is_ the necktie?

2. What color _____ the socks?

is for singular/*are* for plural

3. My boots _____ brown.

4. Susan's sweater _____ blue.

5. Where _____ my shoes?

6. There _____ a coat on the table.

7. Tony's pajamas _____ gray.

8. My socks _____ in the car.

9. Her skirt _____ yellow.

10. Where _____ his black pants?

11. Where _____ my white T-shirt?

C Look at the picture. Check *yes* or *no*.

	YES	NO
1. Sonia is wearing a hat.		✓
2. Michael is wearing shorts.		
3. Gordon is wearing a hat.		
4. Michael is wearing a coat.		
5. Layla is wearing a skirt.		
6. Layla is wearing a dress.		

D Complete the sentences. Look at Activity C. Write *am, is, are, am not, isn't,* or *aren't.*

1. Sonia _____ wearing a coat.

2. Layla _____ wearing a skirt.

3. Michael _____ wearing pants.

4. Layla _____ wearing a dress.

5. Gordon and Michael _____ wearing hats.

6. Gordon and Michael _____ wearing neckties.

E Read the story. Write about you.

   Charlie's favorite color is red. Today he is wearing a blue shirt and black pants. His shoes are brown.

_____ *My favorite color is* _____

_____

_____

_____

_____

_____

_____

_____

At a Department Store

A Find these words in the puzzle. Circle them.

necktie	socks	undershirt	sweater	pants
shorts	shoes	T-shirt	skirt	exit
cashier	boots	jacket	coat	customer

```
W  S  W  L  F  T  S  H  I  R  T  C
P  H  J  A  C  K  E  T  C  S  E  A
A  O  B  O  O  T  S  O  C  K  S  S
N  E  C  K  T  I  E  D  O  I  E  H
T  S  W  E  A  T  E  R  A  R  X  I
S  H  O  R  T  S  Y  E  T  T  I  E
O  C  U  S  T  O  M  E  R  L  T  R
Z  U  N  D  E  R  S  H  I  R  T  J
```

B Put the conversation in order. Number the sentences from first (1) to last (6).

_____ The third floor?

___1___ Can I help you?

_____ They're on the third floor.

_____ That's right.

_____ Yes, I'm looking for children's clothes.

_____ Thanks.

C Circle the correct answers.

1. Where's Claudio?

   A. He's near the entrance.   B. Yes, thank you.

2. Where are Martin and Song?

   A. They're on the first floor.   B. That's right.

3. What's she doing?

   A. On the first floor.   B. She's sleeping.

4. Where are women's coats?

   A. On the first floor.   B. Can I help you?

5. Where is the fitting room?

   A. It's near the exit.   B. She's near the exit.

6. What are Ron and Diana wearing?

   A. We're going into the fitting room.   B. Coats and boots.

D Write the questions.

1. _____ Is he sleeping _____ ?

   Yes, he is. He's sleeping

2. _____ ?

   No, he isn't. He isn't leaving.

3. _____ ?

   Yes, she is. She's trying on the sweater.

4. _____ ?

   No, they aren't. They aren't helping customers.

5. _____ ?

   Yes, they are. They're running.

E Write about you. Use words from the box to complete the chart.

the classroom	pants	the library	socks
the supermarket	shoes	the park	a shirt
a coat	my job	a skirt	a dress
~~school~~	~~a necktie~~		

I AM GOING TO:	I AM WEARING:
school	a necktie

65

Sizes and Prices

A Write the words in order of size: *extra large, medium, small, large.*

_____small_____ < _____ < _____ < _____

B Write the words next to the letters.

S _____   L _____

M _____   XL _____

C Circle the correct answer.

1. What size is that shirt?
   A. blue   B. medium   C. $12.50

2. Is that coat on sale?
   A. Yes, it's 50 percent off.   B. It's a small.   C. It's near the exit.

3. What size is this jacket?
   A. It's a large.   B. It's black.   C. It's a good price.

4. What color are those shoes?
   A. They're large.   B. They're on sale.   C. They're brown.

5. How much is this necktie?
   A. $5.00   B. It's on sale.   C. That's a good price.

6. How much is that dress?
   A. It's a large.   B. It's $25.00.   C. It's near the exit.

D Multiply the numbers.

1. $5 \times 3 = $ _15_

2. $6 \times 3 = $ _____

3. $2 \times 4 = $ _____

4. $3 \times 10 = $ _____

5. $4 \times 12 = $ _____

6. $3 \times 15 = $ _____

E Look at the clothes. Write the amounts of money.

| $10 | 1 blouse = _____
3 x $10 = | ⟶ | $30 |

| $2 | 1 pair of socks = _____
2 x _____ = | ⟶ | _____ |

| $20 | 1 pair of shoes = _____ | | _____ |

| $12 | 1 necktie = _____
_____ x _____ = | | _____ |

| $15 | 1 pair of pants = _____ | | _____ |

How much money is it for all the clothes? TOTAL = _____

F Write about you.

1. I wear a size _____ T-shirt.

2. My jacket is a size _____.

3. My favorite color for pants is _____.

4. _____ is a good price for shoes.

5. The name of my favorite department store is _____.

Identifying Clothes

A Look at the picture. Write sentences about what each person is wearing. List three things.

1   What is Joe wearing?

_____

_____

2. What is Paula wearing?

_____

_____

3. What is Maria wearing?

_____

_____

B Complete the sentences with *a* or *an*.

1. Charles is wearing _____ old coat.

2. Mina is wearing _____ red jacket.

3. There's _____ hole in my sweater.

4. Rudy is cutting _____ piece of paper.

5. Mark is wearing _____ brown shirt, _____ blue jacket, and _____ old pair of pants.

6. I am taking my dress to _____ tailor. He can fix it.

C Look at the labels for Amina's skirt and shirt. Answer the questions

Amina's Skirt

WASH HOT WATER
LINE DRY ONLY
NO BLEACH

M

Amina's Shirt

HAND WASH
COLD WATER
LINE DRY

SMALL

1. What temperature should she wash the shirt in?

   ☐ cold   ☐ warm

2. What temperature should she wash the skirt in?

   ☐ cold   ☐ hot

3. Should she line dry the shirt?

   ☐ yes   ☐ no

4. What size is the skirt?

   ☐ small   ☐ medium

Unit 5: Clothing

Community: Asking for a Refund

A Read the story. Answer the questions.

Karina is a student. She is wearing blue pants. The pants are too big. She wants to return the pants. Casual Clothes is the store. Karina doesn't live near the store. Karina sends the pants back to Casual Clothes in the mail. She sends a form with the pants. She says the pants are too big.

1. What is the student's name? _The student's name is Karina_
2. What is the name of the store? _Casual Clothes._
3. What color are the pants? _The pants are blue_
4. What's the problem? _The pants are too big_
5. Is the store near Karina? _No, it isn't._

B Learn new words. Find and circle these words on the form.

exchange   refund   gift certificate

Step 1
Fill out Customer Information.
Customer Information:

Name: _Karina Stark_
Address: _7325 Meadow Street_
City: _Glendale_   State: _CA_
Daytime phone: _(818) 555-5433_
Zip code: _92101_

Step 2
How would you like us to handle your return?
☐ Exchange item
☑ Refund
☐ Gift certificate

Step 3
List the item(s) you are returning. Include the reason. (See chart below.)

Reason	Description	Color	Price
21	Pants	Blue	$25.00
✓			

Problem:
11 – too small   12 – too short
21 – too big   22 – too long
31 – don't like color
41 – don't like style

C Look at the form in Activity B. Check the information you see.

☐ customer's name   ☐ size of clothes

☐ customer's address   ☐ customer's city

☐ problem with clothes   ☐ customer's school

☐ customer's telephone number   ☐ price of clothes

☐ description of clothes   ☐ how to handle the return

☐ color of clothes

D Your brown coat is too small. It is $50.00. You want a refund. Complete the form.

Step 1
Fill out Customer Information.
Customer Information:
Name: _Andy Huynh_
Address: _556 North Ave 4L_
City: _Fort Lee_   State: _NJ_
Daytime phone: _845-279-8970_
Zip code: _07024_

Step 2
How would you like us to handle your return?
☐ Exchange item
☑ Refund
☐ Gift certificate

Step 3
List the item(s) you are returning. Include the reason.
(See chart below.)

Reason	Description	Color	Price
11	coat	brown	$50.00

Problem:

11 – too small	12 – too short
21 – too big	22 – too long
31 – don't like color	
41 – don't like style	

E Read the conversation. Answer the questions.

A: May I help you?

B: Yes please. I'd like to return these pants. They're too short.

A: Oh, I'm sorry. Do you want an exchange, a refund or a gift certificate?

B: A refund please.

A: Okay. Please fill out this form.

trả lại và lấy lại tiền

1. What is she returning? _She is return these pants._
2. What is the problem? _They're too short._
3. What does she want? _She wants refund_

TAKE IT OUTSIDE: GO TO A STORE. LOOK FOR A SIGN: "RETURN POLICY." WRITE DOWN THE EXPLANATION OF THE RETURN POLICY. BRING IT TO CLASS. TALK ABOUT IT WITH YOUR TEACHER AND CLASSMATES.

Family: Caring for Clothes

A Learn new words. Match the words to the pictures.

1. hand wash _____*d*_____

a.

2. line dry _____

b.

3. dry clean _____

c.

4. machine wash _____

d.

+

5. tumble dry _____

e.

B Look at the labels. Check the correct answers.

WASH HOT WATER
LINE DRY ONLY
NO BLEACH

M

HAND WASH
COLD WATER
LINE DRY

SMALL

DRY CLEAN ONLY

M

MACHINE WASH
WARM WATER
TUMBLE DRY

M

1. Wash the shirt in _____ water.

   ☐ cold   ☐ warm

2. Wash the pants in _____ water.

   ☐ cold   ☐ hot

3. _____ dry the shorts.

   ☐ Line   ☐ Tumble

4. _____ the jacket.

   ☐ Dry clean   ☐ Wash

5. The _____ is a size small.

   ☐ shirt   ☐ jacket

6. _____ wash the shorts.

   ☐ Hand   ☐ Machine

7. _____ wash the shirt.

   ☐ Hand   ☐ Machine

C Write the things you are wearing. Check the way you wash and dry each item.

Clothing	Machine wash?	Hand wash?	Dry clean?	Tumble dry?	Line dry?

Practice Test

DIRECTIONS: Answer the questions. Use the Answer Sheet.

1. Susan wears a large. A large is _____.
   A. L
   B. M
   C. S
   D. XL

2. What size is it?
   A. blue
   B. medium
   C. $7.99
   D. very old

3. How much is it?
   A. blue
   B. medium
   C. $7.99
   D. very old

ANSWER SHEET			
1	A	B	C	D
2	A	B	C	D
3	A	B	C	D
4	A	B	C	D
5	A	B	C	D
6	A	B	C	D
7	A	B	C	D
8	A	B	C	D
9	A	B	C	D
10	A	B	C	D

DIRECTIONS: Look at the price tag to answer the next 3 questions. Use the Answer Sheet.

XL

Men's shirt/green

**Regular price:
$20.00**

Sale price

$12.99

4. What size is it?
   A. small
   B. medium
   C. large
   D. extra large

5. What is the price on sale?
   A. $20.00
   B. 50% off
   C. $12.99
   D. $7.01

6. How much are two shirts?
   A. $40.00
   B. $32.99
   C. $26.98
   D. $25.98

DIRECTIONS: Look at the shirt label to answer the next 2 questions. Use the Answer Sheet on page 74.

MACHINE WASH
COLD
DO NOT BLEACH
LINE DRY
WARM IRON

MADE IN CHINA
100% COTTON
L

7. What size is the shirt?
   A. cotton
   B. cold
   C. dry
   D. large

8. What water temperature should you use to wash the shirt?
   A. cold
   B. cool
   C. warm
   D. hot

DIRECTIONS: Answer the questions. Use the Answer Sheet on page 74.

9. Lilian _____ leaving the store.
   A. be
   B. am
   C. is
   D. are

10. Adam is buying _____ pants.
    A. those
    B. this
    C. that
    D. a

HOW DID YOU DO? Count the number of correct answers on your answer sheet. Record this number in the bar graph on the inside back cover.

Identifying Foods

A Write the words in the correct places in the chart. (More than 1 idea is possible.)

| oranges | bananas | butter | ~~beans~~ |
| grapes | apples | lettuce | carrots |

YELLOW	GREEN	ORANGE
	beans	

B Complete the sentences. Write *is* or *are*.

1. Bananas ___are___ good.
2. Carrots _____ orange.
3. Milk _____ white.
4. I think rice _____ good.
5. There _____ onions on the table.
6. _____ there some butter on the table?
7. Where _____ the tomatoes?
8. There _____ cheese on the bread.

is/are

C Look at Henry's food for this week. Answer the questions.

SUN.	MON.	TUES.	WED.	THURS.	FRI.	SAT.
rice and shrimp	chicken	shrimp and tomatoes	noodles	rice and beans	bread and cheese	chicken and carrots

1. Henry eats _____ on Mondays.
2. On Thursdays, Henry eats _____.
3. Henry eats tomatoes on _____.
4. Henry eats _____ on Wednesdays.
5. Henry eats rice on _____ and _____.
6. Henry eats bread and cheese on _____.

D Make a schedule of your food. Write 1 food for each day.

SUN.	MON.	TUES.	WED.	THURS.	FRI.	SAT.

E Read the story. Check *yes* or *no*.

Henry likes rice. He thinks rice is delicious. Henry doesn't like onions. He thinks onions are terrible. Henry likes oranges and grapes. He doesn't like yogurt.

1. Henry likes yogurt.   ☐ yes   ☐ no

2. He doesn't like rice.   ☐ yes   ☐ no

3. Henry likes grapes.   ☐ yes   ☐ no

4. He doesn't like onions.   ☐ yes   ☐ no

5. He likes oranges.   ☐ yes   ☐ no

F Answer the questions about you. Check *yes* or *no*.

1. Do you like peanuts?   ☐ yes   ☐ no

2. Do you like bananas?   ☐ yes   ☐ no

3. Do you like rice?   ☐ yes   ☐ no

4. Do you like apples?   ☐ yes   ☐ no

5. Do you like onions?   ☐ yes   ☐ no

6. Do you like carrots?   ☐ yes   ☐ no

G Write about you. Use ideas from Activities E and F.

_____

_____

_____

_____

_____

At the Grocery Store

A Make words from the letters.

bakery	restroom	produce section	canned goods
~~fruit~~	vegetables	frozen food	dairy

1. u t i f r   _fruit_

2. k a r y b e   _____

3. f n z o o e d o r f   _____

4. g l e s a v e b e t   _____

5. o d c a o d n s e n g   _____

6. i d y a r   _____

B Complete the sentences. Use words from the box in Activity A.

1. Bread is in the _____ section.

2. _____ and _____ are in the produce section.

3. Milk and cheese are in the _____ section.

C Circle the correct answers.

1. Excuse me. Do you sell cereal?

   A. You're welcome.   Ⓑ Yes, we do.

2. It's in Aisle 1.

   A. Aisle 1?   B. Excuse me.

3. Thanks a lot.

   A. No, we don't.   B. You're welcome.

4. Excuse me. Do you sell peanuts?

   A. No, we don't.   B. Thanks a lot.

5. Do you sell oranges?

   A. Yes. It's in the produce section.   B. Yes. They're in the produce section.

6. Do you sell butter?

   A. Yes. It's in the dairy section.   B. Yes. They're in the dairy section.

D Look at the photos. Write the letters next to the sentences.

A

B

C

1. She is in the produce section. _____

2. She is looking at canned goods. _____

3. She is at the checkout counter. _____

E Check *yes* or *no* about the photos in Activity D.

1. In photo A, the woman is wearing a jacket.   ☑ yes   ☐ no

2. In photo B, the woman is near the fruit.   ☐ yes   ☐ no

3. In photo C, the man is cleaning the floor.   ☐ yes   ☐ no

4. In photo A, the woman has a basket.   ☐ yes   ☐ no

5. In photo C, the woman is a cashier.   ☐ yes   ☐ no

6. The customer in photo B is pushing a cart.   ☐ yes   ☐ no

F Circle the correct words.

1. We buy **banana** / **bananas** in the produce section.

2. I look at **coupon** / **coupons** in the store.

3. Pete buys **milk** / **a milk** in the dairy section.

4. We buy **bread** / **breads** in the bakery.

5. I buy **chicken** / **chickens** in the meat section.

6. Mary buys **butter** / **butters** in the dairy section.

Using Quantity Words for Food

A Match the foods and containers. (More than 1 answer is possible.)

Foods	Containers
1. ___h___ bread	a. jar
2. _____ sugar	b. package
3. _____ milk	c. bag
4. _____ apples	d. bottle
5. _____ cheese	e. box
6. _____ honey	f. carton
7. _____ tomatoes	g. can
8. _____ cereal	h̶. loaf
9. _____ rice	
10. _____ oil	

B Write the name of the container under the picture. Then write 2 foods for each container.

_____	_____	_____	_____
1. ___oil___	1. _____	1. _____	1. _____
2. _____	2. _____	2. _____	2. _____

C Look at the food labels. Answer the questions below.

FRESH SHRIMP	
NET WT	UNIT PRICE	SELL BY
2.0	$6.99/LB	06/08/11
	TOTAL PRICE
	$13.98

FRESH SHRIMP

NET WT   UNIT PRICE   SELL BY
2.0 $6.99/LB   06/08/11

TOTAL PRICE
$13.98

CHICKEN

NET WT   UNIT PRICE   SELL BY
5.0 $3.00/LB   09/15/11

TOTAL PRICE
$15.00

CHEESE

NET WT   UNIT PRICE   SELL BY
.5 $4.50/LB   01/10/11

TOTAL PRICE
$2.25

PEANUTS

NET WT   UNIT PRICE   SELL BY
1.0 $6.99/LB   11/23/11

TOTAL PRICE
$6.99

1. How much is 1 pound of shrimp? _____$6.99_____

2. How much is the package of shrimp? _____

3. How many pounds is the package of chicken? _____

4. How many pounds is the cheese? _____

5. How much is the package of peanuts? _____

6. How much is 1 pound of chicken? _____

7. What is the sell by date for the chicken? _____

8. What is the sell by date for the cheese? _____

9. What is the sell by date for the shrimp? _____

Reading Food Ads

A Read the store flyer. Write the regular prices and the sale prices. Subtract to find the savings.

FOOD	REGULAR PRICE	SALE PRICE	SAVINGS
Milk	$3.00	(2/$5 =) $2.50	$.50

B Write the amounts.

1. What is the amount of milk? _____ 64 ounces _____

2. What is the amount of honey? _____

3. What is the amount of carrots? _____

C Write the amounts another way.

1. 2 lb. = _____ (oz.)

2. 2 quarts = _____ (oz.)

3. 24 ounces = _____ (lb.)

4. 1/2 quart = _____ (oz.)

5. 32 fluid ounces = _____ quarts

> 1 pound (lb.) = 16 ounces (oz.)
> 1 quart = 16 fluid ounces (oz.)

D Match the questions and answers.

Questions	Answers
1. __b__ When do you have milk?	a. I want some bread and cheese.
2. _____ Where do you find fruit?	b. I have milk at breakfast, in the mornings.
3. _____ What do you find in the dairy section?	c. In the produce section.
4. _____ What do you want for lunch?	d. Milk, eggs, and cheese.
5. _____ What do you need to buy?	e. In the bakery.
6. _____ Where do you find bread?	f. I need tomatoes, carrots, and bread.

E Read the store receipt. Write the information.

```
     SAVEMOR'S
    SUPERMARKET


2 lb. @ .50/lb.
     bananas    $1.00

3 lb. @ $2.00/lb.
     chicken    $6.00

cereal            $4.99
     SALE        -$2.00
                  $2.99
     TOTAL        $9.99
```

1. Number of pounds of bananas: ___2___

2. Number of pounds of chicken: _____

3. Price of chicken per pound: _____

4. Regular price of cereal: _____

5. Sale price of cereal: _____

6. Savings on cereal: _____

F Write the questions.

1. _____?

   I shop at Savemor's Supermarket.

2. _____?

   I need bread, milk, and eggs.

3. _____?

   I eat cereal for breakfast.

Family: Nutrition

A Look at the picture. Add a food to each group. Talk with a partner about the foods you eat in each section of the picture.

Grains: Eat at least 3 ounces of whole grains every day. Whole grain bread is better than white bread. Brown rice is better than white rice.

Vegetables: Eat dark green and orange vegetables.

Fruit: Eat different kinds of fruit. Fresh fruit is better than juice.

Milk: Eat low-fat and nonfat milk, cheese and yogurt.

Meat and Beans: Eat low-fat meats, chicken, fish, nuts, and beans.

Source: United States Department of Agriculture

B Look at the two choices. Check the one that is healthier. Then, talk with a partner.

1. apple juice   apples   2. brown rice   white rice

3. red meat   lean fish   4. ice cream   skim milk

C Write 4 sentences about you and people in your family.

EXAMPLES: *I eat brown rice for dinner.*
My father eats pasta at night.

D Read the labels. Answer the questions.

Cranberry Juice Mix 100% Juice	Cranberry Juice Drink	Dinner Rolls	Nine Grain Bread
Ingredients: Cranberry juice, apple juice, white grape juice	**Ingredients:** Sugar, corn syrup, cranberry juice	**Ingredients:** white flour, butter, oil, sugar, yeast	**Ingredients:** whole grain flour, nuts, yeast, honey, vegetable oil
A	**B**	**C**	**D**

1. What foods have sugar? _____

2. What foods include juice? _____

3. What foods have oil? _____

4. What foods have butter? _____

5. What is healthier, the cranberry juice mix or the cranberry juice drink? Why?

_____

6. What is healthier, the dinner rolls or the nine grain bread? Why?

_____

Work: Restaurant Job Descriptions

A Learn new words. Look at the actions in the pictures. Circle the new words in the job descriptions.

take reservations

serve customers

measure ingredients

wash dishes

prepare menu

slice fruits and vegetables

> Note: We often add –*ess* to the job for a woman.

Restaurant Jobs

Host / Hostess or **Maitre d':** takes reservations, greets customers, takes customers to their tables, gives menus.

Waiter / Waitress / Server: takes orders, serves customers, prepares checks.

Head Chef: prepares the menu, orders supplies, cooks, supervises other cooks and kitchen workers.

Manager: opens and closes the restaurant, hires staff, works with suppliers.

Kitchen Worker: measures ingredients, prepares salads, slices fruits and vegetables.

Dishwasher: washes dishes and pots and pans.

B Complete the sentences with the occupations.

1. Ana is a _____. She takes customers orders and brings their food.

2. Sara and Azis are _____. They help the chef in the kitchen. They make salads and slice vegetables.

3. Henry is a _____. He cooks food and prepares the menu for the restaurant.

4. Ly is a _____. She says hello to customers and takes them to a table.

5. Greta is the _____. She hires the other people at the restaurant. She makes work schedules. She also opens and closes the restaurant.

6. Luis cleans the pots and pans. He is a _____.

C Answer the questions about you.

1. Who washes dishes in your family?   _____

2. Where do you buy supplies and groceries?   _____

3. Who slices fruits and vegetables in your home? _____

4. When do you measure ingredients?   _____

5. Where do you make reservations?   _____

D Find someone who…

Someone who . . .	Person's name
works in a restaurant.	
washes dishes every day.	
likes to prepare meals.	
works with customers.	
orders supplies at work.	

Practice Test

DIRECTIONS: Answer the questions. Use the Answer Sheet.

1. Do you want white or wheat bread?
   A. White, please.
   B. Yes, I do.
   C. Chicken.
   D. A sandwich.

2. Where's the cereal?
   A. Yes, we do.
   B. It's in Aisle 3.
   C. That's right.
   D. Thanks a lot.

3. How much is a can of tomatoes?
   A. That's a good price.
   B. That's expensive.
   C. It's in Aisle 4.
   D. 99 cents.

ANSWER SHEET				
1	A	B	C	D
2	A	B	C	D
3	A	B	C	D
4	A	B	C	D
5	A	B	C	D
6	A	B	C	D
7	A	B	C	D
8	A	B	C	D
9	A	B	C	D
10	A	B	C	D

DIRECTIONS: Look at the picture to answer the next 2 questions. Use the Answer Sheet.

$1.00 6 ct.

4. How many eggs are there?
   A. 12
   B. 6
   C. $1.00
   D. 4

5. How much are the eggs?
   A. 12
   B. 6
   C. $1.00
   D. $.06

DIRECTIONS: Look at the food label to answer the next 3 questions. Use the Answer Sheet on page 88.

```
        CHICKEN

NET WT   UNIT PRICE   SELL BY
4.50  $1.99/LB  06/08/11



          TOTAL PRICE
          $8.96
```

6. How much does the package of chicken cost?
   A. $1.99
   B. $4.50
   C. $8.96
   D. $6.08

8. What sell by date is on the package?
   A. 4.50
   B. $1.99
   C. $8.96
   D. 6/08/11

7. How many pounds of chicken are in the package?
   A. 4.50
   B. 1.99
   C. 8.96
   D. 6.08

DIRECTIONS: Answer the questions. Use the Answer Sheet on page 88.

9. What can I get for you?
   A. A pound of cheese.
   B. Aisle 1.
   C. Yes, thank you.
   D. It's on sale.

10. What size is the can?
    A. 2/12/12
    B. 15 ounces
    C. In Aisle 5
    D. $2.50

HOW DID YOU DO? Count the number of correct answers on your answer sheet. Record this number in the bar graph on the inside back cover.

Spotlight: Writing

A Read the recipe. Number the pictures in order from first (1) to last (5).

RECIPE

My Favorite Soup
Lucy Kimball

Ingredients

1 lb. broccoli
1 lb. potatoes
water
salt
pepper

Directions

Wash the broccoli and the potatoes. Cut the potatoes
in quarters and put them in a large pot with water.
Boil the potatoes for about 20 minutes. Add the
broccoli and boil for 3 minutes. Put the broccoli and
the potatoes into a blender. Add some of the water
and blend. Add salt and pepper and serve hot.

Boil the broccoli for 3 minutes.

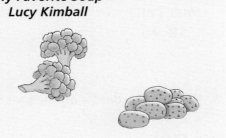

Wash the vegetables.

Blend the vegetables with some water.

Add salt and pepper and serve hot.

Cut up the potatoes
and boil them for
20 minutes.

B Complete the sentences. Match the two parts of each sentence.

Ingredients: pasta, water, peppers, celery, carrots, salt.

Directions:

1. Wash _____ C _____   a. 4 quarts of salted water in a large pot.

2. Cut _____   b. the vegetables to the pasta and cook for 3 more minutes.

3. Boil _____   c. the vegetables in cold water.

4. Cook _____   d. the pasta for 10 minutes.

5. Add _____   e. the vegetables into small cubes

6. Serve hot.

C Choose a favorite recipe. Write the ingredients. Write the directions.

RECIPE

Ingredients

Directions

Identifying Family Members

A Look at the family photo. Read the story. Write the words from the box on the lines.

husband	father	mother	son
brother	niece	sister	son

Pierro — *brother*

Mark — *husband*

Patricia — *mother*

Elizabeth

niece

son

son

This is a photo of everyone in Elizabeth's family. She has two sons. She lives with her husband, Mark, and her children in Paramount, Florida. Elizabeth's mother and father, Patricia and Hugo, live in Paramount, too. She sees them every day. Elizabeth's brother, Pierro, is married. He has two daughters.

B Check *true* or *false*.

1. Elizabeth has two daughters. ☐ true ☑ false
2. She is married. ☑ true ☐ false
3. Elizabeth's mother lives near her. ☑ true ☐ false
4. Elizabeth has a brother. ☑ true ☐ false
5. Elizabeth's brother has a son. ☐ true ☑ false

C Complete the sentences. Write *has, doesn't have, have,* or *don't have.*

1. Elizabeth _____ *doesn't have* _____ a sister.   *has (hat)*

2. Elizabeth and her husband _____ *have* _____ two children.

3. Elizabeth's sons _____ *have* _____ an aunt.

4. Elizabeth and her husband _____ *don't have* _____ grandchildren.

5. Elizabeth's brother _____ *has* _____ two nephews.

D Write the words in the correct order.

1. live / don't / parents / I / with / my
   _____ *I don't live with my parents* _____.

2. have / three / children / We
   _____ *We have three children* _____.

3. doesn't / brother / have / a / She
   _____ *She doesn't have a brother* _____.

4. have / They / grandparents / don't
   _____ *They don't have grandparents.* _____.

5. brother / doesn't / My wife / a / have
   _____ *My wife doesn't have a brother.* _____.

E Look at the chart. Write the number you have in your family.

FAMILY MEMBER	NUMBER	FAMILY MEMBER	NUMBER
mother		father	
sister		brother	
aunt		uncle	
daughter		son	
grandmother		grandfather	

93

Family Responsibilities

A Match the actions and things.

Actions	Things
1. pay	a. the dishes
2. make	b. the trash
3. take out	c. the bills
4. cook	d. the house
5. go	e. the beds
6. clean	f. dinner
7. wash	g. grocery shopping

B Read the schedule and answer the questions.

CHORE	SUN.	MON.	TUES.	WED.	THURS.	FRI.	SAT.
cook dinner	M	C	K	M	C	K	all
wash dishes	C	K	M	C	K	M	all
take out trash	K	M	C	K	M	C	all

Madeline (M), Charmaine (C), and Kristina (K) are roommates. They live together in a house. They work together to do the jobs in their home.

1. Who cooks dinner on Sunday?   _Madeline_____

2. Who washes dishes on Wednesday?   _____

3. Who takes out the trash on Thursday? _____

4. Does Madeline cook dinner on Wednesday? _____

5. Does Kristina wash dishes on Tuesday? _____

6. Does Charmaine take out the trash on Sunday? _____

C Circle the correct words.

Everyone in my family helps at home. I (cook / cooks) dinner on Monday and Wednesday. My mother always (do / does) the laundry. My father (wash / washes) the dishes after dinner. My sisters (take / takes) out the trash. My brothers (clean / cleans) the house. We all (make / makes) our beds in the morning. My mother usually (pay / pays) the bills. (Do / Does) you help at home?

simple present

D Write the words in the correct order.

1. with / you / Do / live / parents / your

   _____ *Do you live with your parents* _____ ?

2. brother / Does / your / near / you / live

   _____ ?

3. Do / children / have / you

   _____ ?

4. grandfather / cook / Does / your / dinner

   _____ ?

5. make / Do / the beds / they

   _____ ?

6. her / brother / take out / Does / the trash

   _____ ?

E Write about you. Who has each family responsibility in your home?

FAMILY RESPONSIBILITIES	WHO DOES IT?
Cook dinner	
Take out trash	
Pay the bills	
Clean the house	
Go grocery shopping	

F Write about who does the chores in your home. Write complete sentences.

_____

_____

_____

Recreation

A Write the words under the photos.

> play soccer   listen to music   play cards   read the newspaper

_____

_____

_____

_____

B Write the actions in Activity A in the order you like them.

1. _____   ❤❤❤❤

2. _____   ❤❤❤

3. _____   ❤❤

4. _____   ❤

C Circle the correct answers.

1. Do you play cards?

   A. Yes, often.　　　　　　B. In the library.

2. Do you play an instrument?

   A. I take pictures.　　　　B. No, I don't.

3. Who in your family plays soccer?

   A. Sometimes.　　　　　　B. My sister.

4. Does your family tell stories?

   A. Two or three.　　　　　B. Yes, often.

5. Do you listen to music?

   A. Yes, sometimes.　　　　B. Yes, you do.

6. Does your father read the newspaper?

   A. Yes, he is.　　　　　　B. Yes, he does.

D Write the words on the lines below. Some words can be used 2 times.

soccer	music	the story	cards
the book	the newspaper	the teacher	an instrument

_____ **play** ____soccer____

_____　　　　_____

_____ **listen to** _____

_____　　　　_____

_____ **read** _____

_____　　　　_____

E Look at the activities on pages 96–97. Tell a partner what you do *always, often, sometimes,* or *never*.

EXAMPLE: I never play cards.

Family Portraits

A Complete the sentences.

ACROSS

1. My son's daughter is my _____.
4. My father's wife is my _____.
5. My mother's husband is my _____.
6. My grandfather is my grandmother's _____.

DOWN

1. My mother's father is my _____.
2. My father's sister is my _____.
3. My brother's son is my _____.

B Write the words in the crossword puzzle below.

C Circle the word that is different in each row.

1. mother   aunt   (cards)
2. father   dishes   brother
3. story   clean   wash
4. pay   son   buy
5. cook   clean   cards
6. wash   read   listen

D Complete the sentences. Write *don't* or *doesn't*.

1. I _____*don't*_____ live here.

2. He _____ have a book.

3. They _____ clean the house.

4. Maria _____ like apples.

5. Fernando and I _____ wash the dishes.

6. You _____ read the newspaper.

7. My parents _____ live with me.

8. My sister _____ work.

9. My aunt and uncle _____ play cards.

10. Ahmed _____ play soccer.

11. We _____ cook dinner.

E Complete the story about Brigitte's family.

   My mother _____ (clean) our house. She _____ (clean / not) every

day. She _____ (work) every day. My father _____ (drive) a bus. He

_____ (go) to work Monday through Friday. I _____ (take) out the

trash. My brother _____ (cook) dinner. My sister _____ (do / not)

anything. She is a baby. My grandmother and grandfather _____ (live) with us. They

_____ (go / not) to school or to work. My grandmother _____ (listen)

to music and _____ (read) books. My grandfather _____ (read) the

newspaper. We _____ (play / not) cards, but we _____ (play) soccer.

F Write about your family. Use compound sentences.

_____

_____

_____

_____

_____

_____

_____

Work: Safe Driving Practices

A Learn new words. Circle the words on the web site.

Motor Vehicles Safe Driving Practices for Employees

child safety seat

Don't drink alcohol.

seat belt

The way you drive says everything about you and your company. Follow these work-related safe driving practices.

Stay Safe

- Use a seat belt at all times.
- Don't take medicine before you drive.
- Don't drink alcohol.
- Use child safety seats for children.

Stay Focused

- Don't eat, play with the radio, or talk on the phone.
- Take a break every two hours.

Don't be Aggressive

- Don't get angry.
- Be polite.
- Plan ahead of time.

B Circle *True* or *False*.

1.	You should always wear a seat belt.	True	False
2.	It's okay to eat when you drive.	True	False
3.	Don't drink alcohol when you drive.	True	False
4.	Children don't need safety seats.	True	False
5.	It's okay to talk on the phone when you drive.	True	False
6.	Don't be angry at other drivers.	True	False
7.	You don't need to take breaks.	True	False

C Answer the questions about you. Then work with a partner. Practice asking and answering the questions.

1.	Do you drive to work?	☐ Yes, I do.	☐ No, I don't.
2.	Do you drive to school?	☐ Yes, I do.	☐ No, I don't.
3.	Do you drive your children to school?	☐ Yes, I do.	☐ No, I don't.
4.	Do you drive every day?	☐ Yes, I do.	☐ No, I don't.
5.	Do you always wear a seat belt?	☐ Yes, I do.	☐ No, I don't.
6.	Do you use child safety seats?	☐ Yes, I do.	☐ No, I don't.
7.	Do you talk on the phone in the car?	☐ Yes, I do.	☐ No, I don't.

TAKE IT OUTSIDE: INTERVIEW A FRIEND, FAMILY MEMBER OR COWORKER. CHECK THE ANSWERS.

Do you always _____	Yes, I do.	No, I don't.
wear a seatbelt in the car?		
put your children in a child safety seat?		
take breaks every two hours?		

Family: Educational Resources

A Learn new words. Look at the documents below. Write the words: *driver's license, birth certificate, report card, immunization record.*

STATE OF TEXAS
DEPARTMENT OF HEALTH
BUREAU OF VITAL STATISTICS
CERTIFICATE OF BIRTH

Birthplace ___ Kingsville / Kingsville Maternity Hospital

Date of Birth ___ March 2, 1975

Full Name of Child ___ Robert Manuel Garza   (male)

Mother's Name ___ Rita Maria Esparazo Garza

Father's Name ___ Roberto Pedro Garza

CALIFORNIA
DRIVER'S LICENSE
EXPIRES: 03-02-12   7805067644   CLASS: 2

ROBERT MANUEL GARZA
1521 MARKET STREET
SAN FRANCISCO, CA
94821

DOB: 03-02-75

HAIR: BRN   EYES: BRN
HT: 5'10"   WT: 160 LBS

Robert Garza

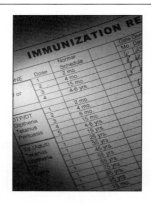

B Read the information. Circle the names of the documents in Activity A.

Enrolling Your Child in School

Are you new to the city? Now is the time to enroll your child in school. School starts on Sept. 1 for all grades (kindergarten through 12th grade). To get started, call the public school system for your city or county. For both public and private schools in this state, you will need to show:

- Your child's birth certificate
- Your proof of residency (for example, your driver's license)
- Your child's past report card if possible
- Your child's immunization record

To enroll in kindergarten, your child must be five by Sept. 1. If you are interested in a pre-K (pre-kindergarten) program for a child younger than five, you should also contact the school system.

After-school day care may be available at some locations.

C Look at the reading in Activity B. Answer the questions.

1. What is one document you can use as proof of residency?

_____

2. What document shows that your child has had all the vaccinations for school?

_____

3. What grades are included in the public school system?

_____

4. How old do students have to be to start kindergarten?

_____

5. What programs are for children who are four or younger?

_____

D Answer the questions about you. Then practice asking and answering with a partner.

1. Do you have children?   _____

2. Do your children go to school?   _____

3. Is there a public school near your home? _____

E Write 3 sentences about someone you know in public school.

EXAMPLE: My daughter goes to a public school. She is in first grade. Her teacher's name is Ms. Hunter.

_____

_____

_____

Practice Test

DIRECTIONS: Read the form to answer the next 5 questions. Use the Answer Sheet.

Parent's Name:	Line 1
Mailing Address:	Line 2
City:	
State:	
Zip:	
Home:	
Business:	
Gender: ○ Male ○ Female	Line 3
Date of Birth: / /	
Marital Status: ○ Married ○ Single	Line 4
Child's Name:	Line 5
Gender: ○ Male ○ Female	
Date of Birth: / /	
Relationship:	Line 6

Terry Coggins lives at 3902 West Peach St. She is single. She has a daughter. Her daughter's name is Pamela.

1. On what line do you check *single*?
   A. Line 1
   B. Line 2
   C. Line 3
   D. Line 4

2. On what line do you write *Terry Coggins*?
   A. Line 1
   B. Line 2
   C. Line 3
   D. Line 4

3. On what line do you check *female*?
   A. Line 1
   B. Line 2
   C. Line 3
   D. Line 4

4. On what line do you write *daughter*?
   A. Line 3
   B. Line 4
   C. Line 5
   D. Line 6

5. On what line do you write *Pamela Coggins*?
   A. Line 3
   B. Line 4
   C. Line 5
   D. Line 6

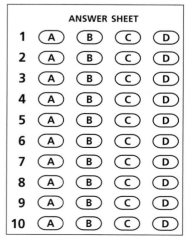

ANSWER SHEET

	A	B	C	D
1	Ⓐ	Ⓑ	Ⓒ	Ⓓ
2	Ⓐ	Ⓑ	Ⓒ	Ⓓ
3	Ⓐ	Ⓑ	Ⓒ	Ⓓ
4	Ⓐ	Ⓑ	Ⓒ	Ⓓ
5	Ⓐ	Ⓑ	Ⓒ	Ⓓ
6	Ⓐ	Ⓑ	Ⓒ	Ⓓ
7	Ⓐ	Ⓑ	Ⓒ	Ⓓ
8	Ⓐ	Ⓑ	Ⓒ	Ⓓ
9	Ⓐ	Ⓑ	Ⓒ	Ⓓ
10	Ⓐ	Ⓑ	Ⓒ	Ⓓ

DIRECTIONS: Answer the questions. Use the Answer Sheet on page 104.

6. Jack and Kay have the same parents. What is Kay's relationship to Jack?
   A. male
   B. sister
   C. nephew
   D. aunt

7. What do they do for fun?
   A. Tell stories.
   B. Take out the trash.
   C. Parents.
   D. Bus driver.

8. What do you pay?
   A. dinner
   B. the dishes
   C. the bills
   D. the laundry

9. What do you do on weekends?
   A. In my house.
   B. I sometimes play soccer.
   C. With my brother.
   D. Yes, I do.

10. Where does your uncle live?
    A. In California.
    B. His wife and children.
    C. She is here.
    D. Never.

HOW DID YOU DO? Count the number of correct answers on your answer sheet. Record this number in the bar graph on the inside back cover.

Parts of the Body

A Write the words from the box on the lines.

| head | shoulder | arm | elbow | hand | leg | knee | back | foot | ankle |

B Make words from the letters.

| wrist | neck | chest | stomach |
| finger | nose | mouth | throat |

1. cekn   _neck_
2. grnife   _____
3. htarot   _____
4. sriwt   _____
5. hotamsc   _____
6. ohtmu   _____
7. thsec   _____
8. soen   _____

C Check *yes* or *no*.

1. People can fly. ☐ yes ☑ no
2. Books can talk. ☐ yes ☐ no
3. Teachers can read. ☐ yes ☐ no
4. Librarians can check out books. ☐ yes ☐ no
5. Computers can cook. ☐ yes ☐ no
6. Children can play soccer. ☐ yes ☐ no

D Complete the sentences about you and your family. Use *can* and *can't*.

1. I _____*can't*_____ cook.
2. My mother _____ play soccer.
3. My father _____ play an instrument.
4. My family _____ speak English.
5. I _____ drive a car.
6. I _____ use a computer.
7. I _____ write my name.
8. I _____ speak Spanish.

E Write the words in the correct order.

1. can / touch / my toes / I

   _____.

2. read / a book / in English / can / I

   _____.

3. They / drive / to school / can't

   _____.

4. can / to the store / We / go

   _____.

5. cook / dinner / He / can

   _____.

6. Giovanna / go / can / to school

   _____.

At a Clinic

A Match the questions and answers.

Nurse's Questions

1. What's the problem?
2. Does your knee hurt, too?
3. Is it broken?
4. Can you touch your toes?

Patient's Answers

a. No, I don't think so.
b. I have an earache.
c. Yes, I can.
d. No, it doesn't.

B Circle the correct answers.

1. What's the problem with Matt?

   A. Matt Harper   B. He has a bad headache.

2. Does your back hurt, too?

   A. No, it doesn't.   B. I have a stomachache.

3. Can you move?

   A. Yes, I think so.   B. I have a fever.

4. I have a sore throat.

   A. Is it broken?   B. Does your head hurt, too?

5. Can you stand on one foot?

   A. No, I can't.   B. That's right.

C Write the problems under the pictures.

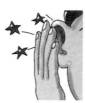

1. _____   2. _____

3. _____   4. _____

D Read the medical history form. Write the information.

Pineville Family Physicians
Medical History

Name: __Peppers__   __Barbara__   __Ann__   Birth Date: __10/17/78__
          Last   First   Middle

Home Address: __1953 Tompkins St.__ __Rowland Heights__ __CA__   __91748__
                    Street Address   City   State   Zip Code

Insurance Information:
Are you covered by insurance?   ☑ yes   ☐ no

If yes, what provider? __Health Plus__

GENERAL QUESTIONS
Do you have a problem with:

1. headaches?   ☑ yes   ☐ no

2. stomachaches?   ☐ yes   ☑ no

3. backaches?   ☐ yes   ☑ no

4. earaches?   ☑ yes   ☐ no

5. sore throats?   ☐ yes   ☑ no

6. fevers?   ☐ yes   ☑ no

Reason for visit: __a terrible cough__

---

1. Patient's name: _____

2. Birth date: _____

3. Problems: _____

4. Insurance company: _____

5. Reason for visit: _____

E Answer the questions about you.

1. How often do you get headaches?   _____

2. Do you sometimes get a sore throat?   _____

3. Do you have a stomachache today?   _____

Understanding Doctors' Orders

A Complete the remedies. Use the words from the box.

1. Put _____ *heat* _____ on it.

2. Take cough _____.

3. Keep it _____.

4. Eat soft _____.

5. Drink _____.

6. Use _____.

medicine
dry
liquids
ear drops
~~heat~~
food

B Read the letters. Underline the problems.

Dear Dr. Dina, **(greeting)**
I get terrible headaches. I can't work or go to school when I have a headache. Help!
　　　　　　　(closing) Sincerely,
　　　　　　　(name) Sick Susan

Dear Sick Susan,
Sometimes you can take aspirin or rest to help a headache. You can also see your doctor. Good luck!
　　　　　　　　　Sincerely,
　　　　　　　　　Dr. Dina

Dr. Dina,
My son has a backache. He hurt his back in soccer. He feels terrible. What should I do?
　　　　　　　Sincerely,
　　　　　　　Worried Mom

Dear Worried Mom,
I think your son will be fine. He should put heat on his back and rest. Call the doctor if he is not OK tomorrow.
　　　　　　　　　Sincerely,
　　　　　　　　　Dr. Dina

Dr. Dina,
My mother has a fever. She also has a cough and a runny nose. I want to help. What can I do?
　　　　　　　Sincerely,
　　　　　　　Daughter
　　　　　　　in Rosemead

Dear Daughter in Rosemead,
Your mother can take aspirin for her fever. She should rest in bed and drink a lot of liquids. You are a good daughter to take care of your mother.
　　　　　　　　　Sincerely,
　　　　　　　　　Dr. Dina

C Match the problems with Dr. Dina's advice in Activity B.

Problems

1. headache

2. backache

3. fever, cough, and runny nose

Dr. Dina's Advice

a. See a doctor, rest, and take aspirin.

b. Take aspirin, rest, and drink liquids.

c. Put heat on it, rest, and call the doctor.

D Write a letter to Dr. Dina. Look at the first letter in Activity B for ideas.

_____, **(greeting)**

_____

_____

_____

_____

(closing) _____,

(your name) _____

E Write the sentences in the correct places in the chart.

See a doctor every year.
Do your homework.
Watch TV every day.
Sleep in class.
Read to your children.

Play with your children.
Drive a car without a driver's license.
Use ear drops for a headache.
Eat healthy food.
Eat ice cream for every meal.

should/shouldn't

THINGS YOU *SHOULD* DO	THINGS YOU *SHOULDN'T* DO

F Make the sentences negative.

should/shouldn't

1. You should go to bed. _____You shouldn't go to bed._____
2. He should see a doctor. _____
3. We should have a party. _____
4. They should pay the bill. _____
5. She should be late. _____
6. I should eat dinner. _____

111

Medicine Labels

A Look at the labels. Write the word under the picture.

prescription medication   over the counter medication

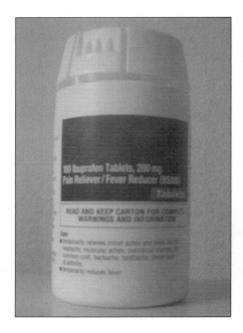

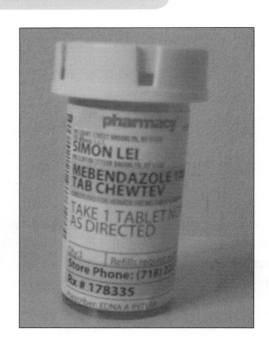

1. _____

2. _____

B Find the words from the medicine bottles in the puzzle. Circle them.

as directed   fever   pain   tablet   pharmacy   store phone   take   warnings

```
G  J  M  L  Y  P  T  A  K  E  C
S  T  O  R  E  P  H  O  N  E  O
A  H  X  Y  P  H  A  T  C  D  G
B  F  A  V  E  A  V  A  F  M  B
F  P  C  I  O  R  M  B  E  N  Y
V  A  W  Q  X  M  C  L  V  I  L
X  I  Y  C  O  A  O  E  E  T  E
A  N  L  E  T  C  N  T  R  P  D
I  C  A  B  N  Y  N  G  S  O  I
C  W  A  R  N  I  N  G  S  X  I
A  S  D  I  R  E  C  T  E  D  F
```

C Put the conversation in order. Number the sentences from first (1) to last (7).

_____ Here you go.

_____ Lei.

_____ What's your last name?

_____ I need to pick up a prescription.

_____ How do you spell that?

_____ It's L - E - I.

____1____ How can I help you?

D Circle the correct answer.

1. What's wrong?
   A. My stomach hurts.   B. This morning at 8 A.M.

2. Are you okay?
   A. They're tablets.   B. No, I don't think so.

3. What's the matter with his foot?
   A. He has a broken ankle   B. He has a toothache.

4. I have a bad headache.
   A. Can you still go to work?   B. Thanks.

5. You should rest.
   A. Thanks, Dr. Janus.   B. Are you okay?

E Circle the correct answer

1. Paul is at the doctor. **He** / **Him** is not feeling well. **Him** / **His** head hurts. **He** / **Him** has a fever. The doctor tells **he** / **him** to take pain tablets.

2. Lara has a sprained ankle. **She** / **Her** is at home. **Her** / **She** ankle hurts.

3. Vivian and Jing are sick. **They** / **Them** are resting. **They** / **Them** take pain relievers every four hours. **They** / **Their** husbands call **them** / **their** every two hours.

4. I don't feel well. **My** / **Me** stomach hurts. **I** / **My** have a headache. **I** / **Me** have a fever, too. I have **my** / **me** medicine. I am watching TV. I am resting.

5. My children and I are sick. The doctor is examining **us** / **we**.

6. Can you bring me the ear drops? I put **them** / **they** in the bathroom.

113

Family: Hand Washing and Hygiene

A Learn new words. Write the phrases under the pictures.

| brush teeth | clip nails | comb hair | floss teeth | take a shower | wash hair |

_____ _____ _____

 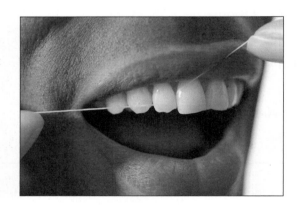 

_____ _____ _____

B Answer the questions about you.

1. When do you usually wash your hair?

_____

2. When do you brush your teeth?

_____

3. When do you floss your teeth?

_____

4. Do you take a shower in the morning or in the evening?

_____

5. How often do you clip your nails?

_____

6. Do you usually brush or comb your hair?

_____

C Read the information. Circle *True* or *False*.

Wash Your Hands

Wash your hands often. When you wash your hands, you stop the spread of germs. Always wash your hands after you use the restroom and before you cook or eat. Follow these steps.

1. Use warm water and liquid soap.

2. Wash for at least 15 seconds.

3. Use a paper towel to dry your hands.

4. Turn off the faucet with the paper towel.

1. You should wash your hands once a day.	True	False
2. You should wash your hands for at least 15 seconds.	True	False
3. You can dry your hands on your shirt.	True	False
4. Turn the faucet off before you dry your hands.	True	False
5. Use a paper towel to turn off the water.	True	False
6. Washing your hands can help you stay healthy.	True	False

Community: Emergency Services

A Learn new words. Read the information.

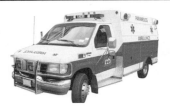

ambulance

An ambulance brings sick or injured patients to a hospital. Sometimes an ambulance takes people from one medical place to another.

emergency room

People go to the emergency room when they are very sick or are hurt. You can go to the emergency room for a broken leg or a heart attack. Don't go to the emergency room for a sore throat.

fire protection services

Call 911 for fire protection services. If you see a fire, fire fighters will help.

police department

Police officers help keep people safe. Call the police if you see a crime, an accident or other problem.

poison control

Some things you eat, inhale, or drink can hurt you, including cleaning supplies, gas, and the wrong medicine. Call a poison control center if someone swallows something dangerous.

disaster services

Disasters are things such as tornadoes, hurricanes, floods, and fires. The government and other organizations help with disasters.

B Look at the pictures. Write the letters of the services that can help.

a. ambulance   b. disaster services   c. fire protection   d. police department

1. _____

2. _____

3. _____

4. _____

C Complete the sentences.

1. A: Someone is stealing my car.

   B: You need the _____.

2. A: Oh, no! My son is drinking the wrong medicine.

   B: Call _____.

3. A: I see a fire.

   B: Call 911. Ask for _____.

4. A: I broke my arm.

   B: You should go to the _____.

Practice Test

DIRECTIONS: Look at the label to answer the next 5 questions. Use the Answer Sheet.

1. What does Extra Bright contain?
   A. bleach
   B. ammonia
   C. flammable
   D. large loads

2. You should avoid contact with:
   A. skin
   B. eyes
   C. washer
   D. water

3. You have young children. Where should you keep Extra Bright?
   A. in their bedroom
   B. under the kitchen sink
   C. in a locked cabinet
   D. in a place that's easy to reach

4. You should not use Extra Bright with _____.
   A. clothes
   B. children
   C. hot water
   D. ammonia

5. You got Extra Bright in your eyes. What should you do?
   A. Call the doctor.
   B. Avoid contact.
   C. Flush with water.
   D. Lie down.

ANSWER SHEET

	A	B	C	D
1	A	B	C	D
2	A	B	C	D
3	A	B	C	D
4	A	B	C	D
5	A	B	C	D
6	A	B	C	D
7	A	B	C	D
8	A	B	C	D
9	A	B	C	D
10	A	B	C	D

Directions to clean clothes:
Fill cap to line. Add to washer. Use more for large loads. Wash as usual. Works in hot or cold water.

Caution: Contains bleach. Avoid contact with eyes. In case of eye contact, flush with water. Do not use with ammonia.

Keep out of reach of children.

DIRECTIONS: Look at the form to answer the next 5 questions. Use the Answer Sheet on page 118.

Injury Checklist

Name of patient: _____ ① _____ Date of birth: _____

Address: _____ City: _____ State: _____ Zip: _____

Sex: ☐ male ☐ female   Marital status: ☐ single ☐ married ☐ divorced

Occupation: _____ ② _____

Date of visit: _____ ③ _____ Time of the visit: _____ ④ _____

Reason for visit: _____ ⑤ _____

Type of injury: ☐ bruise   ☐ burn   ☐ cut   ☐ fracture   ☐ sprain ⑥

Body part injured: ☐ ankle   ☐ arm   ☐ back   ☐ chest   ☐ finger ⑦

☐ hand   ☐ head   ☐ ear   ☐ eye   ☐ leg

Patient signature: _____

6. Tom had an accident. He injured his finger. Where does he check "finger"?
   A. space 1   B. space 3
   C. space 5   D. space 7

7. Dotty cut her leg. Where does she check "cut"?
   A. space 2   B. space 4
   C. space 6   D. space 8

8. Where do you write your occupation?
   A. space 2   B. space 4
   C. space 6   D. space 8

9. Mrs. Moony visits the doctor on October 5, 2011. Where do you write the date?
   A. space 1   B. space 3
   C. space 5   D. space 7

10. Where do you write the person's name?
   A. space 1   B. space 3
   C. space 5   D. space 7

HOW DID YOU DO? Count the number of correct answers on your answer sheet. Record this number in the bar graph on the inside back cover.

Spotlight: Writing

A Read paragraphs A and B below. Find these words. Then answer the question at the end of each paragraph.

Find these words with **S**.
s _h_ _o_ _u_ _l_ _d_
s ___ ___
s ___ ___ ___ ___ ___ ___ ' ___
s ___ ___ ___
s ___ ___ ___ ___

Find these words with **C**.
c _a_ _r_ _e_
c ___ ___ ___ ___ ___ ___ ___ ___
c ___ ___ ___ ___ ___
c ___ ___ ___ ___ ___ ___ ___
c ___ ___

OPINION POLLS

A

Should the government provide free hospital care? I asked ten classmates this question. Four classmates think the government should provide free hospital care. Six classmates think the government shouldn't provide free hospital care. In my opinion, the government should provide free hospital care. All sick people need help. What do you think?

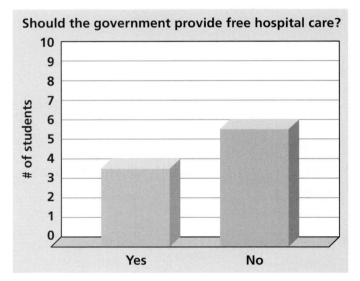

Should the government provide free hospital care?

B

Should parents choose wives* for their sons? I asked ten classmates this question. Three classmates think parents should choose their sons' wives. Seven classmates think sons should choose their wives. In my opinion, parents should choose wives for their sons. Parents understand their children. They can make good decisions. What do you think?

*Note: The plural of *wife* is *wives*.

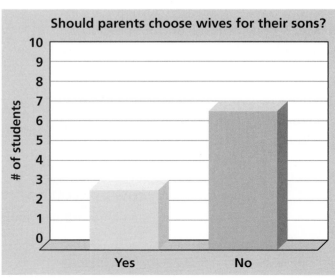

Should parents choose wives for their sons?

B Write this paragraph again. Use a piece of paper. Indent the first sentence.

Should children work outside the home? I asked ten classmates this question. Eight classmates think children shouldn't work. Two classmates think children should work. In my opinion, children shouldn't work. They should study. What do you think?

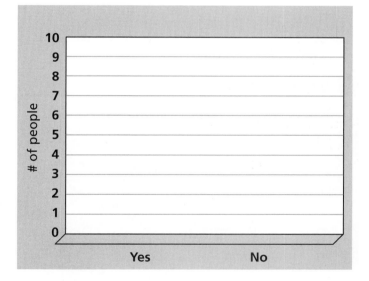

FOCUS ON WRITING: Indent a Paragraph

Indent the first sentence in a paragraph.

EXAMPLE:

My name is Ann. I like to watch TV, read books, and go to school. I don't like to go to the supermarket.

C Choose 1 opinion question. Interview 10 people. Draw a bar graph. Write the results of your opinion poll. Remember to indent.

OPINION QUESTIONS

• Should schools provide free lunches?

• Should schools provide computers to all students?

Unit 9: House and Home

Inside Your Home

A Write about your home. Write the words in the correct place in the chart. More than 1 idea is possible.

bathtub	bed	table	sofa
bookcase	stove	refrigerator	closet
lamp	dresser	rug	toilet
cabinet	smoke alarm	shower	chair

BATHROOM	BEDROOM	DINING ROOM	KITCHEN	LIVING ROOM
bathtub				

B Circle *true* or *false*.

1. There is a coffee table in the room.
   true   false

2. There are two lamps in the room.
   true   false

3. There isn't a sofa.
   true   false

4. There is a bookcase.
   true   false

5. It is a kitchen.
   true   false

6. There aren't people in the room.
   true   false

C Write about the room in Activity B. Use *There is/isn't* and *There are/aren't*.

This room is a _____

_____

_____

D Put the words in the correct place in the chart.

old	sofa	coffee table	desk	rug	big	~~three~~	two
large	white	medium-sized	lamp	yellow	small	new	red

NUMBER	SIZE	AGE	COLOR	NOUN
three				

E Write sentences about things you have in your home.

1. _____ *I have a large brown sofa.* _____

2. _____ .

3. _____ .

4. _____ .

5. _____ .

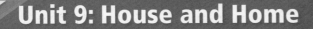
At Home

A Look at the photo. Check the things you see.

☐ pool

☐ garden

☐ garage

☐ carport

☐ front yard

☐ driveway

☐ patio

B Match the things and the places.

Things	Places
1. car	a. garage
2. flowers	b. patio
3. grass	c. yard
4. chairs	d. pool
5. water	e. garden

C Complete the sentences. Use the words from Activity B.

1. You can put your _____ *car* _____ in your garage.

2. You can plant _____ in your garden.

3. You can mow _____ in your yard.

4. You can have _____ on your patio.

5. You should put _____ in your pool.

D Circle the correct words.

simple past of *be*

1. Last week I (am / **was**) sick.
2. Today (**is** / was) Friday.
3. Yesterday (is / **was**) Sunday.
4. We (are / **were**) late to work last night.
5. They (**are** / were) in the library now.
6. In our old apartment, the table (is / **was**) in the living room.

E Look at the photo and read the ad. Check *yes* or *no*.

1289 Tynedale St., Alhambra

Move in now and enjoy this 4-bedroom home. Formal living room with fireplace, dining room, kitchen with breakfast area, 3 baths, and 2-car garage.

Open House
Come and see it!

Today   2:00 P.M.–4:00 P.M.
(626) 555-5440

1. There is a fireplace.
☐ yes   ☐ no

2. It has 5 bedrooms.
☐ yes   ☐ no

3. It has 3 bathrooms.
☐ yes   ☐ no

4. There is a garage.
☐ yes   ☐ no

5. People can see the house at 2:00 P.M.
☐ yes   ☐ no

F Write sentences about your home.

EXAMPLE: *My home has a* __*driveway*__ *. It doesn't have a* __*garage*__ .

1. _____

_____

2. _____

_____

3. _____

_____

Accidents at Home

A Write the past forms of the verbs.

1. clean   _____
2. slip   _____
3. study   _____
4. like   _____
5. call   _____
6. need   _____
7. work   _____
8. dance   _____
9. want   _____
10. trip   _____

B Complete the sentences. Use the past forms of the verbs in Activity A.

1. I can't come to work today. I _____ in the bathtub.

2. Last night, I _____ for my English test.

3. We _____ all night at the party. Today, I'm tired.

4. They _____ on the project for 12 hours yesterday.

5. Henry _____ on a rug and fell.

6. We _____ a doctor yesterday to make a doctor's appointment.

C Match the questions and answers.

Questions	Answers
1. What happened to Kathy?	a. They fell down the stairs.
2. Is he OK now?	b. Yes, I think so.
3. What happened to the children?	c. He cut his hand with a knife.
4. How many people got hurt at the game yesterday?	d. Three.
5. What happened to Peter?	e. She slipped in the shower.

D Learn new words. Find and circle the words in the reading.

bicycle	helmet	carpet	toys	tape	protect

Keep your children safe: Prevent accidents

Follow these steps to protect your child from falls:

1. Don't put chairs near windows.
2. Close and lock windows when children are alone in the room.
3. Put tape on rugs and carpet so they can't slip.
4. Keep toys and other things away from your stairs.
5. Tell your child to wear a helmet when riding a bicycle.

A

B

E Write the number of the step that matches the photo in Activity D.

Photo A: Step _____   Photo B: Step _____

F Check *yes* or *no*.

1. You should put toys on the stairs.   ☐ yes   ☐ no
2. You shouldn't have chairs near windows.   ☐ yes   ☐ no
3. You should put tape on rugs and carpet so they don't slip.   ☐ yes   ☐ no
4. Children shouldn't wear helmets when they ride bicycles.   ☐ yes   ☐ no
5. You should close windows when children are alone in the room.   ☐ yes   ☐ no

G Write one thing you do to prevent accidents in your home.

_____

_____

127

Housing Ads

A Find these words in the puzzle. Circle them.

1. stove
2. bed
3. toilet
4. apartment
5. condo
6. lamp
7. sofa

8. closet
9. yard
10. patio
11. garage
12. pool
13. sink
14. room

```
s  i  n  k  c  s  t  o  v  e
g  t  o  i  l  e  t  h  u  l
s  n  f  p  o  o  l  a  m  p
o  p  o  t  s  v  w  c  k  m
f  a  y  b  e  d  m  o  p  r
a  p  a  r  t  m  e  n  t  o
g  a  r  a  g  e  y  d  i  o
z  b  d  p  a  t  i  o  a  m
```

B Match the abbreviations and the words.

Abbreviations	Words
1. apt	a. month
2. ba	b. apartment
3. bed	c. garage
4. gar	d. bathroom
5. nr	e. near
6. mo	f. bedroom

C Complete the sentences. Use the simple past form of a verb in the box.

call   like   need   ~~play~~   rent   slip

1. We _____played_____ in the yard.

2. She _____ a new coat.

3. We _____ an apartment near the school.

4. Nick _____ the condo.

5. You _____ me.

6. I _____ in the shower this morning.

D Complete the conversations. Write questions with *May I, Can I,* or *I would like to.* Pay attention to the punctuation at the end of the sentences.

1. A: _____ see the garage.

   B: No Problem.

2. A: _____ visit the local school?

   B: Of course. I can set up an appointment for you.

3. A: _____ look at the kitchen?

   B: Certainly. It's this way.

4. A: _____ rent this apartment.

   B: Great!

5. A: _____ write a check?

   B: Yes, that's perfect.

E Write requests or offers that you can use when you look at a house or an apartment for rent. Tell a partner.

1. _____ *May I see the backyard?* _____

2. _____

3. _____

4. _____

5. _____

6. _____

Work: Safety Equipment

A Learn new words. Find and circle the words in the reading.

harness	protective equipment	ear plugs	machinery
hard hat	coveralls	safety glasses	gloves

Safety Rules

1. Do not wear loose clothing around machinery.

2. Wear protective equipment: safety glasses, ear plugs, gloves, hard hat, coveralls, and harness when necessary.

3. Wear appropriate clothing and shoes.

4. Fire doors and aisles must be clear. Do not block aisles or exits with boxes.

5. No running.

6. Clean up spilled liquid and oil.

7. Turn off machines when you are not using them.

B Match the protective equipment and the body parts.

Protective Equipment	Body Parts
1. safety glasses	a. ears
2. harness	b. whole body
3. coveralls	c. eyes
4. hard hat	d. hands
5. gloves	e. head
6. ear plugs	f. back

C Complete the sentences. Use the words from the box.

slip   fall   cut   hurt   leave

1. You should clean up spilled liquid or oil so you don't _____ on the wet floor.

2. Workers need to keep the exits and aisles clear so people can _____ the building.

3. People wear hard hats because something could _____ on their heads.

4. Workers should wear harnesses when they lift heavy things or they can _____ their backs.

5. Sometimes workers _____ their hands on the machines.

D Circle the correct words.

Last week, Rita (slips /(slipped)) on the floor at work. There (is / was) some oil on the floor. She (injures / injured) her back. Rita (is / was) better now. She (is / was) back at work. Her supervisor (calls / called) a meeting yesterday with all the workers. Now everyone (is / was) careful. They (don't want / didn't want) to fall and get hurt.

E Write about you. Write a story about a time you got hurt. Answer these questions.

1. What happened to you?

2. When did you get hurt?

3. What part of your body got hurt?

4. What did you do?

_____

_____

_____

_____

_____

TAKE IT OUTSIDE: INTERVIEW A FAMILY MEMBER, FRIEND, OR COWORKER. ASK THE QUESTION. WRITE THE ANSWER.

What is 1 safety rule you have at work or school?

_____

_____

_____

Community: Evacuation Procedures

A Read the information about fire procedures at school and look at the map.

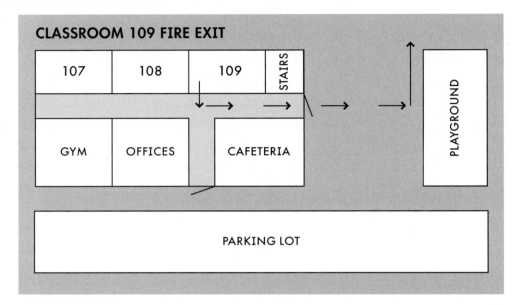

CLASSROOM 109 FIRE EXIT

| 107 | 108 | 109 | STAIRS |

| GYM | OFFICES | CAFETERIA |

PLAYGROUND

PARKING LOT

FIRE EVACUATION PROCEDURES
- If you see a fire, pull the fire alarm.
- Don't use elevators in a fire. Use the stairs.
- Follow the exit route shown on the map.
- The last person out of the classroom should close the door.
- If you are not in the classroom, go to the nearest exit.
- Go to the designated area outside the building and wait.

B Read each sentence. Circle *yes* or *no*.

1. You should use the elevators in a fire.   yes   (no)

2. You should call 911 if you see a fire at school.   yes   no

3. You should follow the fire exit route.   yes   no

4. Students in room 109 should go to the parking lot.   yes   no

5. The last person out of the classroom should close the door.   yes   no

6. You should go home and wait if there is a fire at school.   yes   no

7. You should stay in the classroom during a fire at school.   yes   no

Bonus Question: Where should you go if there is a fire at your school? _____

C Read the earthquake procedure information. Answer the questions.

Earthquake Procedures

Drop, Cover, and Hold procedures inside the classroom:
1. Drop down to your knees and get under furniture (desk, table, chair, etc.).
2. Hold on to furniture with one hand. Place the other hand over the back of your head and neck.
3. Keep your body under the furniture and wait for instructions.

Drop, Cover, and Hold procedures outside the classroom:
1. Get away from all buildings, power lines, light poles, trees, and structures.
2. Drop down to your knees, bend forward, and cover your head and neck with your hands.
3. Stay where you are and wait for instructions.

Drop, Cover, and Hold procedures to and from school:
1. Get away from all buildings, power lines, light poles, trees, and structures.
2. Get into the Drop, Cover, and Hold position if possible.

1. You are in the classroom. Where should you go during an earthquake?

   A. outside   B. under a desk or table   C. to the windows

2. What should you do during an earthquake?

   A. get on your knees   B. stand up   C. sit in a chair

3. You are outside during an earthquake. What should you do?

   A. go to a building   B. go under a tree   C. stay in an open area

4. What body part should you cover with your hand?

   A. your foot   B. your neck   C. your knee

D **Conversation Challenge.** Write the words from the box on the correct lines.

leave	Pull	Go
wait	Near	

> ***Useful Expressions**
>
> *to ask for the next step*
> Now what do we do?
> Then what?
> What's next?

A: Oh, no! There's a fire in the trash can.

B: _____ the fire alarm.

A: OK, **now what do we do*?**

B: _____ outside and _____. Don't _____.

A: Where do we meet the rest of the class?

B: _____ the playground.

A: I'm glad you know what to do.

B: Just read the procedures on the wall. Then you will know, too.

Practice this conversation with a partner. Use different Useful Expressions.

Practice Test

DIRECTIONS: Look at the ads to answer the next 5 questions. Use the Answer Sheet.

1	For Sale Condo, 3 bed, 2 bath, pool, garage	2	House for Rent 4 bed, 2.5 bath, garage, nr schools and shopping
3	For Rent Large, sunny apt., near downtown 2 bedrooms, 1 bath, no pets $650/month	4	For Rent Beautiful House 5 bed, 3 bath, patio gar., pool $1,200/month

1. Which ad is for an apartment?

   A. 1

   B. 2

   C. 3

   D. 4

2. Which ad is for a condo?

   A. 1

   B. 2

   C. 3

   D. 4

3. Which ad has 3 bathrooms?

   A. 1

   B. 2

   C. 3

   D. 4

4. Which place has 4 bedrooms?

   A. 1

   B. 2

   C. 3

   D. 4

5. Which place has a patio?

   A. 1

   B. 2

   C. 3

   D. 4

ANSWER SHEET

	A	B	C	D
1	A	B	C	D
2	A	B	C	D
3	A	B	C	D
4	A	B	C	D
5	A	B	C	D
6	A	B	C	D
7	A	B	C	D
8	A	B	C	D
9	A	B	C	D
10	A	B	C	D

DIRECTIONS: Look at the bar graph to answer the next 5 questions. Use the Answer Sheet on page 134.

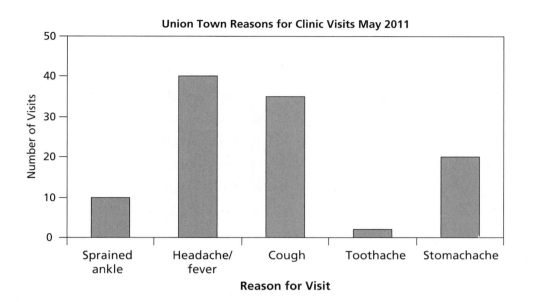

Union Town Reasons for Clinic Visits May 2011

6. In May, _____ people visited the clinic for a sprained ankle.
   A. 0   B. 20   C. 50   D. 10

7. In May, 40 people visited the clinic for _____.
   A. headache/fever   B. stomachache   C. cough   D. toothache

8. in May _____ people visited the clinic for a toothache.
   A. 3   B. 10   C. 15   D. 0

9. In May, 35 people visited the clinic for a _____.
   A. headache/fever   B. stomachache/toothache   C. cough   D. sprained ankle

10. In May, _____ people visited the clinic for a stomachache.
   A. 22   B. 32   C. 40   D. 12

HOW DID YOU DO? Count the number of correct answers on your answer sheet. Record this number in the bar graph on the inside back cover.

Identifying Occupations and Skills

A Match the jobs and actions.

Jobs	Actions
1. chef __i__	a. takes care of children
2. child care worker ____	b. takes care of plants
3. construction worker ____	c. uses a computer
4. home healthcare provider ____	d. drives a truck
5. landscaper ____	e. lifts heavy things
6. mechanic ____	f. builds buildings
7. mover ____	g. fixes cars
8. office manager ____	h. repairs toilets
9. plumber ____	i. cooks food
10. truck driver ____	j. takes care of sick people

B Read the story. Answer the questions.

Claire is 16 years old. She is looking for a job. She wants to work after school. Claire can drive a car. She got her driver's license last month. She can take care of children. She took care of her sister's children for a week last year. Claire is in 11th grade. She learned to use a computer in school.

1. What 3 things can Claire do?

_____

_____

2. Does Claire want a full-time job?

_____

_____

3. What job(s) do you think Claire can do?

_____

_____

C Answer the questions about you.

1. Write 3 things you can do.

_____

2. What kind of job do you want in the future?

_____

3. List 3 jobs you did in the past.

_____

4. Do you want to work 40 hours a week?

_____

D Write about you. Use your answers in Activity C to write a paragraph.

_____

_____

_____

_____

_____

_____

_____

E Complete the sentences. Use the past tense of the verbs in parentheses.

1. Gilda _____ (is) a home healthcare provider. She _____ (take) care of sick people in their homes.

2. Tony _____ (is) an office manager. He _____ (manage) a busy office of 120 people.

3. Sam _____ (is) a construction worker. He _____ (build) schools and libraries.

4. Larry _____ (is) a truck driver. He _____ (drive) a large truck.

5. Marina _____ (is) a babysitter. She _____ (take) care of children today.

Understanding Forms of Identification

A Write the abbreviations next to the words.

| FT | PT | eves | hr | exp. | ~~req'd~~ |

1. required _____req'd_____   4. full-time _____

2. hour _____   5. experience _____

3. evenings _____   6. part-time _____

B Read the ads. Complete the sentences.

FT Office Manager
Professional and
friendly person
needed for busy
office. Exp. req'd.
Computer and office
skills req'd. Benefits.
$400/week. Fax resume
to: (626) 555-9702

Landscaper
Exp'd FT landscaper
needed. Driver's
license req'd. $18/hr.
Good benefits.
Apply in person to:
Parker Homes
112 North Ave.
Pasadena, CA.

Childcare Worker
PT childcare worker
needed. 1 year
exp. req'd. $9.50/hr
Call Angie:
(310) 555-2234

1. The _____childcare worker_____ job is part-time.

2. The _____ job pays $18 an hour.

3. You need computer skills for the _____ job.

4. You need a _____ for the landscaper job.

5. If you want to apply for the _____ job, you need to go in
   person to the office.

6. If you want to apply for the _____ job, you need to call Angie.

7. If you want to apply for the _____ job, you need to fax a resume.

C Take notes on the ads in Activity B. Complete the chart.

JOB	FT OR PT	$	WHAT IS REQUIRED	HOW TO APPLY
Office manager				Fax resume
		$18/hour		
	Part-time			Call

D Answer the questions. Use the information in Activity B.

1. Mark got the landscaper job in Activity B. How much will he earn in 1 week working 40 hours?

   _____

2. Mark gets an extra $9 ($18 + $9) an hour when he works on Saturdays.
   How much will he earn for 8 hours on a Saturday?

   _____

3. Tony wants to be an office manager. He will work 40 hours a week. How much money will he earn in 1 hour?

   _____

4. Julia got the job as a childcare worker. How much money will she earn for 10 hours of work?

   _____

5. Angie works with Julia, but she makes $3 more an hour.
   How much does Angie earn in 10 hours?

   _____

E Put the conversation in order. Number the sentences from first (1) to last (5).

_____ Do you have experience?

_____ Can you come in for an interview tomorrow at 10 A.M.?

_____ Yes, I do. I was a mechanic for 3 years in Mexico.

___1___ I'm calling about the ad for a mechanic.

_____ Yes. I'll be there at 10:00 A.M.

F Choose the correct answer.

1. The job starts at 9:00 AM Monday
   A. I won't be late!   B. I arrived on time.

2. Please bring two forms of I.D.
   A. I will bring my diver's license and passport.   B. What time is lunch?

3. What time can you be here for an interview?
   A. I'll come at 11:00 AM   B. When do I start?

4. Could you please fax me your resume?
   A. I will do it this afternoon.   B. When can I call you?

At a Job Interview

A Read the job interview tips. Check *true* or *false* below.

www.howtogetajob.com

HOME

TIPS

EMAIL

Interview Tips

- Dress neatly.
- Arrive early.
- Bring paper and a pen.
- Know the name of the interviewer and how to pronounce it.
- Be polite to everyone.
- Do not chew gum or smoke.
- Ask questions if you don't understand something.
- Wait 1–2 seconds before you answer a question.
- Listen carefully.

In a job interview,

1. you should wear dirty clothes.	☐ true	☑ false
2. you should smoke if you want to.	☐ true	☐ false
3. you shouldn't chew gum.	☐ true	☐ false
4. you should ask questions.	☐ true	☐ false
5. you should wait a little before you answer.	☐ true	☐ false
6. you shouldn't say the interviewer's name.	☐ true	☐ false

B Match the questions and answers.

Interviewer's Questions

1. Where are you working now?
2. Do you like your job?
3. What did you do before that?
4. When was that?
5. Did you like that job?
6. Do you have experience?

Job Applicant's Answers

a. Yes, I was an office manager for 2 years.
b. Yes, I do. It's a great job.
c. At BigMart.
d. Yes, very much. The people were nice, and I learned to use a computer.
e. I was a salesclerk at Best Books.
f. April 2010 to January 2011.

C Answer the questions about you.

1. Are you working now?

_____

2. What did you do before?

_____

3. When was that?

_____

4. Do you have experience as an office manager?

_____

5. What skills do you have? (for example, *I can drive a truck*.)

_____

6. What do you do well? (for example, *I listen carefully*.)

_____

D Where do you think they work? Write the jobs next to the places.

home healthcare provider	construction worker	landscaper
child-care worker	chef	plumber
mover	mechanic	truck driver

1. A-1 Trucking _____

2. Caring for Kids _____

3. Anthony's Italian Restaurant _____

4. Green Thumb Landscaping _____

5. National Moving Company _____

6. Builders, Inc. _____

7. The Car Doctors _____

8. Sinks, Toilets, and Tubs _____

9. Feel Better at Home _____

An Amazing Story

A Learn new words. Find and underline the words in the story.

married	got his first job	died
started racing motorcycles	became the owner	decided to go back to school
started teaching	was born	finished college

OBITUARIES
August 10, 2012

Mr. Douglas Nichols, 95, of Pasadena, died August 9, 2012, at Mercy South Hospital. He was born December 22, 1916, in Pine Bluff, Arkansas, the son of Lewis and Maria Nichols. He lived in Pasadena from 1978 until his death. He married Sophia Wasawski in 1960.

Early in life, Doug showed great mechanical ability. He fixed watches in first grade. As he got older, he started to fix cars, airplanes, and motorcycles.

He got his first job as a motorcycle mechanic in 1934. In 1962, Doug became the owner of the Nichols Motorcycle Company. He wasn't happy just fixing motorcycles— he wanted to ride them, too. He started racing motorcycles in 1965. Doug also loved boats and began racing speed boats in 1967. He set a world speed boat record in Florida in 1971.

When Doug was 60 years old, he decided to go back to school. He finished college in 1982. He started teaching science in 1985 and retired in 1990. He then volunteered as a teacher until 2000.

Survivors include his wife, Sophia, and sons, Ivan and Gregory.

B Number the events in Activity A from first (1) to last (6).

_____ Douglas Nichols died.

_____ Doug got his first job.

__1__ Doug Nichols was born.

_____ He married Sophia.

_____ Doug became the owner of Nichols Motorcycle Company.

_____ He finished college.

C Write the events from the reading in Activity A on the timeline below.

Year	Event
1916	_____
1934	_____
1960	_____
1962	_____
1965	_____
1971	_____
1982	_____
1990	_____

D Complete the timeline for you. Write when you were born and other important things.

Year	Event
_____	_____
_____	_____
_____	_____
_____	_____
_____	_____

E Complete the sentences. Write *am, is*, or *are*.

1. I _____*am*_____ going to apply for a job.

2. She _____ going to help me with my application.

3. _____ he going to call you today?

4. The students _____ going to go to the library tomorrow.

5. Do you think it _____ going to rain tonight?

6. _____ you going to finish college?

F Write 3 things you are going to do in the next year. Use *am going to* in your sentences.

_____

_____

_____

_____

Family: Goals

A Take the quiz.

What are your goals for the future?

Check the things you would like to do in the next 5 years.

- ☐ get married
- ☐ have a child
- ☐ start college
- ☐ get a better job
- ☐ learn to speak English better
- ☐ meet new people

- ☐ spend more time with family
- ☐ go to another country
- ☐ buy a car
- ☐ buy a house
- ☐ read more books

☐ _____
_____ (your idea)

B Read the story. Underline Tatiana's goals.

Tatiana is from Peru. She came to the United States in 2006 with her daughter, Claudia. Tatiana is working in a clothing store now, and Claudia goes to school. Tatiana loves to cook and wants to be a chef. She wants to work in a nice restaurant, so she is going to start classes at the community college in September. She is going to study how to be a chef. Tatiana is saving money for her classes. She needs $1,000. Tatiana is going to work some extra hours at the store, but she wants Claudia to have child care after school. Tatiana is going to ask her sister to take care of Claudia after school.

C Complete the chart.

TATIANA'S GOAL	WHAT TATIANA IS GOING TO DO TO REACH HER GOAL
Be a chef	
	Work extra hours at the store
Have child care for Claudia	

D Choose 3 of your goals from Activity A. Write them in the chart.

YOUR GOAL	WHAT YOU ARE GOING TO DO TO REACH YOUR GOAL

TAKE IT OUTSIDE: INTERVIEW A FAMILY MEMBER, FRIEND, OR COWORKER. ASK THE QUESTIONS. COMPLETE THE CHART.

Name: _____

What are two goals you have for the next year?	What is one thing you will do to reach your goal?

Work: Performance Evaluations

A   Read Carla's job evaluation. Complete the chart.

JOB PERFORMANCE EVALUATION

Employee: Carla Diaz   Date: 12/10/2012

Job requirement	Above the requirements	Meets the requirements	Does not meet the requirements	Comments
1. Comes to work on time			✓	Carla is often late.
2. Works well with others		✓		She is friendly with other employees.
3. Is a hard worker		✓		She always finishes her work.
4. Dresses neatly		✓		Carla always looks neat and professional
5. Follows directions			✓	Carla doesn't always listen carefully to directions.

Supervisor's signature: _____ *Joseph Hart* _____

Employee's signature: _____ *Carla Diaz* _____

THINGS CARLA DOES RIGHT	THINGS CARLA SHOULD IMPROVE

B   You are a supervisor. Do you want to give Carla a job promotion? Why or why not?

_____

_____

 Talk to a partner and share your answer.

C Circle *True* or *False*. Then compare answers with a partner.

To get a job promotion:

1. You need to go to work on time.   True   False

2. You need to be a hard worker.   True   False

3. You need to wear shorts and T-shirts.   True   False

4. You need to follow directions.   True   False

5. You don't need to listen.   True   False

D Look at the pictures. Write the names next to the descriptions.

Marina

Helena

1. This worker dresses neatly and works hard. _____

2. This worker doesn't dress neatly and isn't organized. _____

Who do you want to promote? Why?

TAKE IT OUTSIDE: INTERVIEW A FAMILY MEMBER, COWORKER OR FRIEND. COMPLETE THE CHART.

What job do you want in 5 years?	What is one requirement for that job or promotion?	Who can you talk to about that job or promotion?

Practice Test

DIRECTIONS: Look at the ads to answer the next 5 questions. Use the Answer Sheet.

A.

Childcare Worker
FT or PT. M-F, 7 a.m. – 5 p.m.,
no exp. req'd. Need responsible
and friendly person.
Apply in person:
Tiny Toddlers
1619 West Avenue

B.

Chef
Mario's Pizzeria
Full-time, 3–11,
Tuesdays–Saturdays
1 year exp. req'd.
To apply, call:
(202) 555-6200
Ask for Tham.

C.

Plumbers and helpers
with experience needed
for new company. FT.
Great pay, benefits.
Driver's license req'd.
Call (608) 555-7925.

D.

Landscaper
FT landscaper needed
at Health Inc. 7 a.m. to 3:30.
Benefits. 2 years min.
exp. Apply in person,
1900 Selwyn Rd.

	ANSWER SHEET			
1	A	B	C	D
2	A	B	C	D
3	A	B	C	D
4	A	B	C	D
5	A	B	C	D
6	A	B	C	D
7	A	B	C	D
8	A	B	C	D
9	A	B	C	D
10	A	B	C	D

1. Tina needs a part-time job. Which one is good for her?
   A. Job A
   B. Job B
   C. Job C
   D. Job D

2. Which job is in the afternoons and evenings?
   A. Job A
   B. Job B
   C. Job C
   D. Job D

3. Which job includes great pay?
   A. Job A
   B. Job B
   C. Job C
   D. Job D

4. John has to go to class at 4:00 P.M. Which job ends before then?
   A. child-care worker
   B. chef
   C. plumber
   D. landscaper

5. Which job does not require experience?
   A. child-care worker
   B. chef
   C. plumber
   D. landscaper

DIRECTIONS: Look at the job application to answer the next 5 questions. Use the Answer Sheet on page 148.

Job Application Form

(PLEASE PRINT)

First Name _____ Middle Initial _____ ①

Last Name _____ ②

Birth Date ___6/23/70_____

Present Address _____ ③

City _____ State _____ Zip Code ___95652____

Phone Number ___(916)555-4938_____

• Are you currently employed?   ☐ Yes   ☐ No   ④
• Do you have a valid driver's license? ☑ Yes   ☐ No   ⑤
• Do you have access to an automobile?   ☑ Yes   ☐ No

• Number of hours/week desired: _____ ⑥
• Days and A.M./P.M. hours available:

	Mon.	Tues.	Wed.	Thurs.	Fri.	Sat.	Sun.	
A.M.	☑	☑	☑	☑	☑	☑	☐	⑦
P.M.	☐	☐	☐	☐	☐	☐	☐	

6. On what line do you write your first name?
   A. Line 1   C. Line 3
   B. Line 2   D. Line 4

7. On what line should you write your address?
   A. Line 1   C. Line 3
   B. Line 2   D. Line 4

8. Lidia is working now, but she wants a new job. Where can she say this?
   A. Line 1   C. Line 3
   B. Line 2   D. Line 4

9. Ben can only work on Wednesday and Thursday nights. Where can he say this?
   A. Line 4   C. Line 6
   B. Line 5   D. Line 7

10. Where do you check that you have a driver's license?
   A. Line 4   C. Line 6
   B. Line 5   D. Line 7

HOW DID YOU DO? Count the number of correct answers on your answer sheet. Record this number in the bar graph on the inside back cover.

Spotlight: Writing

A Read the stories below. Find these words.

Find these words with H.
h _a_ _p_ _p_ _e_ _n_ _e_ _d_
h __ __
h __ __ __
h __ __ __ __ __
h __'__
h __ __ __ __
h __ __ __ __ __

Find these words with M.
m _e_ __
M __
m __ __ __ __
m __ __ __ __ __ __
M __ __ __ __

STORIES

Victor

Last week was a good week for me. Two good things happened. I got a new job and we bought a new TV. Only one bad thing happened. My daughter fell down and cut her hand. She's okay now.

Angela

Last week was pretty good for me. Three good things happened. I bought a new dress and I went to a movie. I also got a new cell phone. Nothing bad happened last week.

Amy

Last week wasn't very good for me. One bad thing happened. My husband got sick. Now he's in the hospital. Two good things happened, too. My friends came to my house and helped me. My mother also came from Miami. She is taking care of my children.

B Complete the paragraph below. Use the information in the Idea List.

IDEA LIST	
Good Things	**Bad Things**
I earned some money.	I had a problem at work.
I sold my car.	I got a parking ticket.
I ate at a good restaurant.	I had a headache for two days.

FOCUS ON WRITING: Idea Lists

Before you write a paragraph, write your ideas in a list. Then write your paragraph.

Last week was pretty good for me. Three good things happened. I _____ *earned some money* _____
and I _____. I also _____.
Three bad things happened. I _____ and I _____.
I also _____.

C What happened to you last week? Make a list. Then write your paragraph.

IDEA LIST	
Good Things	**Bad Things**

_____

_____

_____

_____

_____

_____

_____

_____

All-Star Student Book 1 / All-Star Workbook 1

Correlation Table

Student Book Pages	Workbook Pages	Student Book Pages	Workbook Pages
PRE-UNIT		**UNIT 4**	
2–3		46–47	46–47
		48–49	48–49
UNIT 1		50–51	50–51
		52–53	52–53
4–5	2–3	56–57	54–57
6–7	4–5	56–57	54–57
8–9	6–7	58–59	58–59
10–11	8–9		
14–15	10–13	**UNIT 5**	
14–15	10–13		
16–17	14–15	60–61	62–63
		62–63	64–65
UNIT 2		64–65	66–67
		66–67	68–69
18–19	16–17	70–71	70–73
20–21	18–19	70–71	70–73
22–23	20–21	72–73	74–75
24–25	22–23		
28–29	24–27	**UNIT 6**	
28–29	24–27		
30–31	28–29	74–75	76–77
		76–77	78–79
UNIT 3		78–79	80–81
		80–81	82–83
32–33	32–33	84–85	84–87
34–35	34–35	84–85	84–87
36–37	36–37	86–87	88–89
38–39	38–39		
42–43	40–43		
42–43	40–43		
44–45	44–45		

Student Book Pages	Workbook Pages	Student Book Pages	Workbook Pages
UNIT 7		**UNIT 9**	
88–89	92–93	116–117	122–123
90–91	94–95	118–119	124–125
92–93	96–97	120–121	126–127
94–95	98–99	122–123	128–129
98–99	100–103	126–127	130–133
98–99	100–103	126–127	130–133
100–101	104–105	128–129	134–135
UNIT 8		**UNIT 10**	
102–103	106–107	130–131	136–137
104–105	108–109	132–133	138–139
106–107	110–111	134–135	140–141
108–109	112–113	136–137	142–143
112–113	114–117	140–141	144–147
112–113	114–117	140–141	144–147
114–115	118–119	142–143	148–149

Credits

All multiple photos on page, credits read left to right on page or top to bottom in a column.

Page 5: Comstock Images/Alamy; **10:** Photolink/Getty; Blend Images/Jupiter Images; RF/Corbis; PhotoLink/Getty; Erica S. Leeds; **26:** Photolink/Photodisc/Getty; Ilene MacDonald/Alamy; John A. Rizzo/Getty; RF/Corbis; Steve Mason/Getty; TongRo Image Stock/Alamy; **41:** Photodisc; **42:** RF/Corbis; Comstock; Don Farrall/Getty; The McGraw-Hill Companies; **43:** Tetra Images/Alamy; Ingram Publishing/ FotoSearch; The McGraw-Hill Companies, Ken Karp photographer; Burke/Triolo/Brand X/Jupiter Images; **53:** Steve Satushek/Getty; Stock 4B RF; Pixland/AGE/Fotostock; **54:** Getty/Blend; **55:** Nick Rowe/Getty; **63:** Stockbyte/Getty; **68:** Stockbyte/Punchstock; **70:** Ryan McVay/Getty; **71:** Digital Vision/Getty; **72:** C. Squared Studios; C. Lee/PhotoLink/Getty; PhotoLink/Getty; Christian Darkin/ Alamy; Ingram Publishing/Alamy; BananaStock/Alamy; **73:** The McGraw-Hill Companies; The McGraw-Hill Companies; Ingram Publishing/Fotosearch; Studiohio; **79:** Getty/Photodisc; The McGraw-Hill Companies, Andrew Resek; Jack Hollingsworth/Getty; **85:** John A. Rizzo; C.Squared Studios/Getty; Photodisc/Punchstock; Rozenbaum/F.Cirou/Photoalto; Ingram Publishing/Superstock; Bananastock/Punchstock; Ingram Publishing/Alamy; The McGraw-Hill Companies; **86:** RF/Corbis; Bananastock/Punchstock; StockFood/ Superstock; Bananastock/Punchstock; Andersen Ross/Getty; Bananastock/Punchstock; **92:** Getty; **96:** Rubberball/Getty; Keith Brofsky/ Getty; Bananastock/Alamy; BrandX Pictures/Punchstock; **100:** Comstock/Alamy; Stockdisc/Getty; D. Falconer/Photolink/Getty; ©Nova Development; **102:** RF/Corbis; Don Farrall/Getty; **103:** DigitalVision/Getty; Bananastock/Punchstock; **114:** Bloom Productions/Getty; Photodisc/Getty; Photoalto/Punchstock; ImageSource; RF/Corbis; Comstock Images/PictureQuest; **115:** C.Sherburne/Photoline/Getty; The McGraw-Hill Companies; **116:** Comstock Images; RF/Corbis; RF/Corbis; Tom Carter/Alamy; Darrin Klime/Getty; Photodisc/Getty; U.S. Air Force photo technician, Sgt. Richard Freeland; **117:** Mark Gibson/Getty; RF/Corbis; ©Nova Development; Comstock/AGE Fotostock; **122:** Photodisc/Getty; **124:** BrandX Pictures; **125:** BrandX Pictures; **127:** Bananastock/Alamy; The McGraw-Hill Companies; **130:** RF/ Corbis; **136:** SW Productions/Photodisc/Getty; **142:** Creatas Images; **144:** Medio Images; **147:** Ingram Publishing/Alamy; Bananastock/ age Fotostock.